How to Make and Use
COMPOST

How to Make and Use
COMPOST
THE ULTIMATE GUIDE

Nicky Scott

green books

First published in 2009 by

GREEN BOOKS
Foxhole, Dartington
Totnes, Devon TQ9 6EB
www.greenbooks.co.uk

Design by Stephen Prior

Drawings and Illustrations by Nicky Scott except page 191,
'Germination', © Virginia Lee. Thanks to Garden Organic for allowing us to
use the drawings on pages 59, 94 and 168.

All photographs by Nicky Scott except:
Black and white section: pages 35, 42, 93, 118 and 144 © Amanda
Cuthbert; page 97 © Jane Hirst; page 157 (bottom) © Growing Our Future;
page 148 © Community Composting Network; page 160 © Ridan; page 164
(right) © Dale Unsworth; page 170 © Carolyn Anderson; page 47 ©
ARticulate.
Colour section: pages 1, 2 (top), 6 (top) and 8 © Amanda Cuthbert; page 4
(bottom) © Dale Unsworth; page 5 (top) © Carolyn Anderson.

Printed in the UK by TJ International, Padstow, Cornwall.
The text paper is made from 100% recycled post-consumer waste; the
covers from 75% recycled material.

All prices quoted in this book are accurate at the time of printing (November
2009).

ISBN 978 1 900322 59 1

CONTENTS

DEDICATION

I would like to dedicate this book to the countless millions of microorganisms that are so often maligned – it's the same old story: a few bad bacteria give all the rest a bad name. Like my Dad always said, about the advert that declares the product "kills 99 per cent of germs – dead!", "It's the other one per cent that kills you!"

ACKNOWLEDGEMENTS

Thanks to Dick Kitto for early composting experiences and for suggesting I spend time at the Henry Doubleday Research Association, and thanks to Lawrence Hills, Patrick Hughes, Pauline Pears, Alan Gear and my fellow students Pat, Ali and Margaret for making it such a special time. Thanks to all the wonderful crazy people, far too numerous to mention individually I'm afraid, whom I've met in the composting world since the community composting phenomenon started, especially the Community Composting Network team and members – and all those schoolchildren, members of the public, friends, colleagues and workshop attendees who've asked me awkward questions that I've had to go away and think about! Also thanks to the Compost Doctors for their endless enthusiasm and dedication in finding new ways to compost food waste. To Jim Frederikson from the Open University and Phil Wallace for reading through the manuscript and suggesting changes. To Terry Cooper for coming along at the last minute and giving some invaluable advice. To Tian for all the Bowen therapy that enabled me to keep typing. Finally, thanks to all my friends and family, especially Yuli, for putting up with me while I was writing this book and coming up with lots of useful suggestions. Also to Amanda, Alethea and Steve for having to dredge through my manuscript and beat it into something intelligible.

INTRODUCTION

Given the right conditions, anything that lived recently, and quite a few things that were living hundreds of years ago, can be composted.

I've been fascinated by compost and all that it does for decades now, probably ever since I had a Saturday job at Powlings Compost in Ipplepen, Devon. Dick Kitto, who owned the business, went out collecting all kinds of organic 'waste' products locally, from blood and hair from the Harris Bacon factory in Totnes to spoiled fruit and veg from the shops and market; all kinds of things were blended with used mushroom compost, mixed and stacked into great heaps to compost down, and finally sieved and weighed into little bags with the distinctive Powlings' robin logo.

I thought it was great that Dick built a business from stuff that would otherwise have been thrown away, and later on he encouraged me to become a student at the Henry Doubleday Research Association (now Garden Organic). Whilst there I started to learn how compost helps create and maintain healthy soils, why this is the foundation of growing organically, and just why it is so important that we all become organic gardeners.

We made large compost heaps, bulking them up with bought-in strawy manures, and I loved the thrill of seeing that steam rising off them on cold spring mornings. I was introduced to the compost toilet system there too. One of the great things about being at Henry Doubleday's was the constant experimentation, and that inspired me to experiment with different composting and mulching systems, which I continue to do today: there's always more to find out.

We are increasingly aware of the need to live within the resources of the planet we live on, and composting has a big part to play. Everything that has been made falls into one of two recycling loops. The first is a 'technological' loop for all metals, plastics and other man-made substances. We can't do anything apart from separate this material out for recycling, but we can do a lot with the second loop – the 'bio' loop of biodegradable stuff.

Anything that once lived:

- can be used as fuel
- can be anaerobically digested to produce energy and soil conditioner
- can be composted.

This book is about the second two options. Nearly all of us can compost at least some of the clippings from our garden or by-products from our cooking. Once you separate out all the compostable stuff that was going into your dustbin you won't have such a heavy and smelly bin to deal with and you will be transforming it all into the most wonderful substance: compost.

There are a lot of myths about things you cannot compost, but in fact the process is easy, very satisfying and fun. If all the materials that, supposedly, we cannot compost were actually non-biodegradable then the world would now be completely overwhelmed with orange peel, rhubarb leaves, grass cuttings, dog poo, cooked food and so on.

The seemingly conflicting advice from different books, leaflets and other received wisdom on composting can be confusing; I hope this book will help clear up these muddied waters. However, composting is not an exact science and so it is not always possible to give absolutely clear instructions, as the compost process is a living, breathing natural system and so many variables are at work. Often when giving advice I find myself saying, 'Hmm, well, that depends on . . . '. I hope this book will enable you to think through and solve any particular situation you face.

The A–Z Guide in Part Two will, I hope, give you the answers to your composting questions, and it also includes explanations of all the composting terms you'll find in the main part of this book. The Resources section (Part Three) includes many suggestions for further reading, as well as details of relevant organisations and contact details for suppliers of all the products mentioned in the book. There are some fascinating topics that I have not covered in depth, which you can explore further with these resources – for example, biodynamic composting, biochar and compost teas. For those who are interested in taking things further I have included chapters on community composting and on composting food waste on a larger scale, in your community or school.

I'm always amazed when people tell me they don't make compost because it is such hard work and takes too much time. I find composting so satisfying and therapeutic that I don't notice the time, and as for hard work, well you can put a lot of effort into turning heaps, but my main task is digging out finished compost – a job I relish as I know how much my plants will benefit from it.

Most of the hard work in any composting system is done by the worms. Where would we be without worms? It's said that Charles Darwin spent more time studying worms than developing his theory of natural selection. He was studying the earth-dwelling worm, *Lumbricus terrestris*, which burrows deep into the soil, not the compost-dwelling species of worms, e.g. *Eisenia fetida*, but together the two main types of worm form the basis of a healthy and vibrant organic growing system.

I hope this book will inspire you to become as fascinated and enthusiastic about compost as I am. When my sister heard I was writing my third book on composting she was amazed: "Surely you've said everything there is to say?" But I'm learning new things all the time; the world of compost and how it relates to a healthy soil is a fascinating, complex story. This book is just the tip of the iceberg!

So why not give it a go? There are just so many plus sides to making compost – building healthy soil and plants, saving money, locking up carbon and much more, and by reading this book you will quickly become a compost expert your-self. It is really very simple, very satisfying, and fun.

I have worked with compost for nearly forty years and, although I'm not a scientist, I have tried and tested just about everything I've written about. Nearly every compost expert and practitioner I talk to has strong opinions, and experts will give contradictory advice from time to time, so I doubt I would be able to please all the experts all the time. But I have realised that if you understand the basic concepts of composting, consider the qualities of the materials that you want to compost, and are willing to experiment and observe what is going on, then you will become an alchemist, transforming a rather unlikely assortment of materials into that wonderful black gold that is compost . . .

PART ONE

CHAPTER 1

WHY MAKE COMPOST?

"Why would you want to deny the Earth your cauliflower stalk?" – Satish Kumar

At the end of a meal, many leftovers go straight into the bin along with any peelings, etc. from preparing the food. We currently throw away a third of the food we buy, but the tide is turning and more and more people want to grow their own food in healthy soil, and reduce their waste, which is why making compost is so important.

Whatever type of soil you have, compost will improve it. I've heard people talk about how compost is only a 'soil conditioner', as though somehow this was not really important. I think they mean that compost does not add much in the way of nutrients to the soil, but this is not the point. Soil conditioning really means adding humus to the soil. Humus is stable organic matter in the soil and it acts like 'glue', holding on to nutrients and water. In effect humus adds life back to the soil: doing this is the most important thing that we can do for the soil and it's ridiculously easy.

Compost has some nutrient value too, mostly held by the microbes that have proliferated during the composting process. The following are just some of the benefits of adding compost to your soil.

Healthy soil

> *Compost feeds your soil, which feeds your plants.*

Compost adds life in the form of microorganisms

Using compost on your soil will dramatically increase the amount of life in that soil – both life that is visible to the naked eye and, more importantly, life that can be seen only through a microscope. The addition of compost builds a healthy soil and so boosts the microbial activity, which provides food for hundreds of thousands of different species of fungi, bacteria and other organisms; these microorganisms are also food for a whole range of other organisms, which in turn are fed off by predators. What we can see when we look at compost are the creatures, mini-beasts on the macro scale; you will need a magnifying glass to see the very small ones, but many are obvious and well known to us. See 'More wildlife', page 18, for more on this.

> *The soil microbes feed your plants and protect them from pests and diseases.*

Crucially, this microscopic world is cycling nutrients from the compost materials into a form that the plants in our gardens can easily assimilate, and holding them in the soil until the plants need them. Of all the soil organisms the worm is the one that we all recognise as invaluable for creating a healthy soil, and it does indeed possess almost miraculous powers – both the compost-dwelling species and the larger soil dwellers – but in fact it is the whole complex web of life in the soil that is kept vibrant by regular additions of compost.

> *There are over 600 million beneficial bacteria in just one gram of healthy soil (about a level teaspoonful).*

Compost changes the physical structure of the soil

The humus that remains when compost has been further broken down in the soil coats the soil particles and creates the crumb structure that allows the exchange of gases and liquids. So in sandy soils compost increases not only the water-holding capacity but also the nutrient-holding capacity of the soil. In clay soils it flocculates the clay particles – it gathers the minute particles of clay together, again into a crumb texture.

Compost buffers the soil pH

> *Compost 'buffers' the extremes of acidity and alkalinity in a soil.*

Healthy, humus-rich soils 'buffer' the extremes of acidity and alkalinity – humus doesn't actually change the pH, but it enables plants to grow that would otherwise be intolerant of the degree of alkalinity or acidity of your soil.

Compost adds air

> *Compost opens up clay soils.*

Compost helps open up clay soils and compacted soils, enabling them to breathe. Soils that cannot breathe become anaerobic (without air), and without air organic matter in the soil can ferment, with anaerobic microorganisms producing all kinds of by-products toxic to plants, such as alcohol.

Compost reduces the need to water

> *Compost (and humus) improves the water-holding capacity of free-draining sandy soils.*

In free-draining soils, compost holds moisture. If soils cannot hold water then plants wither and die, so increasing the water-holding capacity of soil is a fundamental and dramatic advantage. When the compost has finally been broken down by the life in the soil, a fraction of stable carbon remains as colloidal particles (i.e. humus), which hold on to water molecules.

Less need for fertilisers

> *The tiny (colloidal) particles of humus create a massive surface area in the soil. This whole area holds on to nutrients which would otherwise be washed into the subsoil, beyond the reach of the plants' roots.*

Humus improves the cation exchange capacity (known as CEC) in soils. Put crudely, as well as holding moisture within its particles (absorption), humus has a negative electrical charge, which attracts positively charged nutrients – cations – holding on to them at the surface of the particles (this is known as *ad*sorption), making them freely available to the plants. Clay soils have strong cation exchange capacity and can be extremely fertile as a result; however, they compact easily and without enough aeration they are not productive. The addition of compost adds the necessary air.

Most plants growing in a healthy soil form symbiotic associations with the soil mycorrhizal fungi. These fungi take compounds exuded by the plant, and in exchange the plant takes minerals and nutrients from the fungi. Some plants also form associations with bacteria: the most well known of these are the azobacters, which help leguminous plants take up nitrogen.

The micro flora and fauna in the soil also hold on to and cycle nutrients around the plants' roots, helping to build the soil ecosystem.

Conversely, adding chemical fertilisers and pesticides to soils kills off soil micro flora and fauna. Chemical fertilisers are salts, which are more 'salty' than sea salt, and too much salt will kill off most plants. Furthermore, herbicides and fungicides will kill off other soil organisms; it can be the surfactants (e.g. soap, which is often used to break the water tension), not the active ingredients, that smother and kill the microbes.

Less need for pesticides

Healthier plants mean there is less need for toxic pesticides.

Adding compost and compost tea to soils and plants enables them to resist all kinds of pests and diseases. It is not really within the scope of this book to go into this fascinating area, but all kinds of tests have been done using compost and compost teas, and just how compost helps prevent pests and diseases is becoming more widely understood.

The soil food web is incredibly complex, and it is the soil organisms themselves that are supplying the nutrients in exactly the right form and location to the plant, right to its feeder roots. Bacteria form a protective layer around the plant root hairs, preventing viruses and diseases from getting in. The mycorrhizal fungi also form a barrier around the roots, so that they can exchange nutrients with the plants. What goes on in healthy soil is quite amazing and worth several books in its own right. One of the best contemporary authorities on this area is Elaine Ingham; her website www.soilfoodweb.com is well worth a visit.

Less need to dig

You can never have too much compost in your garden. Clay soils are heavy work to dig, but spreading generous amounts of compost on the surface enables you to sow and plant into this layer, leaving the earthworms to do the digging. Sandy and peaty soils are easier to dig, but digging accelerates the 'burning up' of organic matter in the soil and so it is also good to add compost on the surface. Even if you have a beautiful friable loamy soil, too much digging will disturb the soil ecology, chop up earthworms and can result in soil being compacted, waterlogged and airless. Compost helps to counteract this, but in my opinion it is better to dig as little as possible and to add compost to the surface instead. If you aspire to being a 'no-dig' gardener, you need as much bulky organic matter as you can get, in the form of compost or well-rotted farmyard manure to set up the system in the first place. (See Chapter 6 for how to set up a no-dig garden.)

Carbon sequestration

> *Compost locks up carbon.*

Well-made compost becomes humus, which consists of long stable carbon chains with properties that are still not fully understood. This carbon is locked up in the soil for a very long time, as long as the soil is not ploughed or dug up; if it is, the carbon will combine with atmospheric oxygen and be released as carbon dioxide (CO_2) gas.

Less waste

Think of all the reusable or recyclable materials that we put out for collection. We cannot reprocess glass bottles and tins at home but nearly all of us can make compost and thereby eliminate the need for many lorries having to truck all that material either to be composted centrally or, worse, incinerated. With landfill sites filling up, local authorities have been bringing in recycling and compost collections, but even the best local authorities can divert only about half of the waste from landfill or incineration. The wastage of food is still huge; around 20 per cent of all waste is food and about a third of that waste is food thrown out, still unwrapped, within its sell-by date.

It is obviously far better to eat food than to waste it, but even the preparation of fresh vegetables generates a certain amount of waste in the form of peelings and tops and tails – and, unless this is home composted, it has to be dealt with by local authorities. But why give this precious resource to the council to deal with when we can transform it ourselves into compost?

More wildlife

By creating a living compost to feed your soil you are also feeding a whole food chain, right up to the top predators. A healthy soil will have a thriving worm and invertebrate population, which is food for many birds and other animals.

The compost heap itself is full of life – indeed I like to think of it as a living organism in its own right. Compost heaps become a magnet for all kinds of creatures, including some bigger ones. Predatory beetles move in and hunt for food, larvae and smaller creatures; frogs and toads do likewise, as do slow worms and grass snakes, which love the warmth in a heap. Birds will visit to pick off insects, invertebrates and larvae, and bats will visit at night. For wildlife value alone it's worth making compost, and the wildlife benefits continue through to the soil and the ecosystem you are building and maintaining by adding compost and avoiding chemical fertilisers and pesticides.

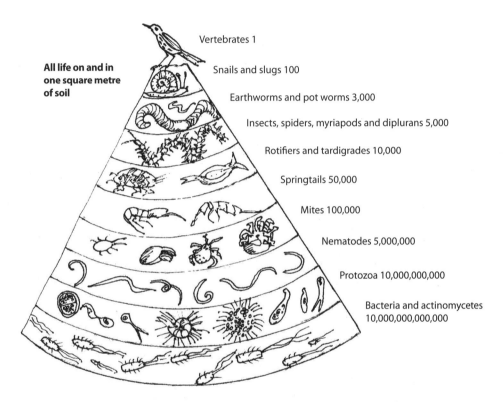

All life on and in one square metre of soil

Vertebrates 1

Snails and slugs 100

Earthworms and pot worms 3,000

Insects, spiders, myriapods and diplurans 5,000

Rotifers and tardigrades 10,000

Springtails 50,000

Mites 100,000

Nematodes 5,000,000

Protozoa 10,000,000,000

Bacteria and actinomycetes 10,000,000,000,000

Saving money

Making compost at home saves money in so many ways. You don't have to buy in compost and growing media, or fertilisers – you can make them yourself.

CHAPTER 2

HOW DOES IT WORK?

Everything that once lived will start to decompose when it dies unless it is preserved in some way by being frozen, pickled, dried, fermented or salted, etc. The microorganisms that decompose dead animals and plants mostly need air, water and warmth to be active. Some of them manage without air, and there are many examples of specialist microbes (extremophiles) that survive in extreme situations.

We are all familiar with the process of rotting – whether from fruit spoiling in the fruit bowl or a fallen tree covered with fungi in a forest. The process of decomposition is happening all the time in the environment, and our soils contain millions of different species of microorganisms in every gram; in fact healthy soil is a more complex ecosystem than a rainforest.

Composting is an artificial acceleration of this decomposition, utilising the same natural process. You need materials high in carbon (the 'browns' – dry, often woody, materials – dead plant material, stems, twigs, chippings, autumn leaves, paper and cardboard, etc.) layered or mixed with materials high in nitrogen (the 'greens' – often wet, sappy materials – grass cuttings, fresh weeds, peelings and skins from the kitchen, urine and manures, etc). The drier materials provide air, either through hollow stems acting like snorkels or, as in the case of twigs and sticks, by creating an internal structure to a heap that allows air and water to pass through freely. The green, wet materials provide the water, which is released as the cell walls break down.

The right balance of these materials provides the perfect environment for an explosion of microbial populations. The whole secret of compost making is to set up this ideal environment for the bacteria, fungi and other creatures that are involved in the decomposition process. They thrive in a moist but not waterlogged environment, with plenty of air: ideally everything is coated with water but there are air spaces in between.

The concept of composting is really simple: once you really take on board that composting is a living, dynamic, natural process then I think you stop thinking of your heap as a kind of dustbin and more as the living, breathing entity that it actually is – a bit like a pet really!

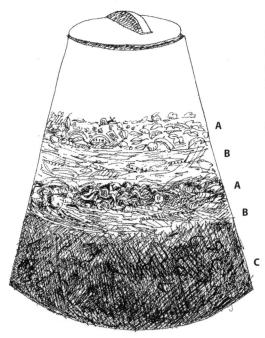

Layering in the compost heap

A   Thinner layers of soft green material with

B   Thicker layers of 'browns' – hard structural and soft absorbent materials.

C   Material maturing and being mixed up by worms.

If you constantly remind yourself of these simple but vital needs of your compost heap, then you will make good compost. If you forget them – well, everything decomposes given time, so what's the worst that can happen? Actually the worst that can happen is a smelly anaerobic (airless) mess that produces toxic leachate – but after reading this book that is *not* what you are going to create!

The four-word mantra

Air Water Food Warmth   Air Water Food Warmth   Air Water Food Warmth

These four basic requirements are the same for us humans and pretty much every life form on the planet, so the mantra shouldn't be hard to remember. What you are doing when you construct an aerobic (with-air) compost heap is creating the right environment for the billions of microorganisms that make the compost happen. Their food is the materials that you put on the heap.

Air

It is most important to think in terms of whether the material you put on your heap will add air or water. A happy heap will have a balance of the two, just like a squeezed-out sponge: the whole surface area is coated in water but there are air spaces in between. If the pile is too dense, squeezing out all the air, or the air spaces get filled up with water, then all the beneficial life forms in the compost heap are not going to survive and will be replaced by the 'bad' microbes – the anaerobic (without-air) ones that are responsible for all the bad odours you get from putrefying substances. This is bad news for your compost and if you put this material on your plants it can be toxic to them.

So, creating air spaces in the compost is vital.

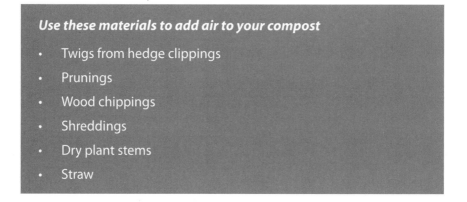

Use these materials to add air to your compost

- Twigs from hedge clippings
- Prunings
- Wood chippings
- Shreddings
- Dry plant stems
- Straw

These materials all serve to open up denser, wetter materials and allow air through. People often want to keep these things out of their compost because of the subsequent 'nitrogen robbery' that occurs when woody material is incorporated into the soil (see Chapter 6, page 83), but it is absolutely vital to maintain airflow throughout the heap, and the problem of uncomposted woody chunks is a minor concern.

Water

The microorganisms that we want to dominate the compost heap are all aerobic (with-air) organisms that nevertheless also need water to live. If we create a dense, wet, anaerobic (without-air) heap then only anaerobic organisms (predominately anaerobic bacteria) will survive, and create unpleasant smells. If your compost heap smells bad then it isn't really composting, it's fermenting or anaerobically digesting. (However, this anaerobic process can be controlled in a positive way – see the Bokashi system in Chapter 4, page 56).

Peelings on their own with no structural materials quickly go slimy and smelly.

Use these materials to add water to your compost

- Fresh fruit and vegetable peelings
- Green leaves – fresh weeds and soft hedge prunings
- Grass cuttings
- Tea leaves
- Coffee grounds

It is important to include materials that will add water to your compost, but beware of adding too much wet stuff – with small domestic heaps there is often a surfeit of over-wet material without anything to absorb it or let the air through.

Use these materials to absorb water from your compost

- Envelopes (remove the windows first)

- Sawdust

- Half-rotted straw – partially rotted materials become more absorbent

- Half-rotted woodchippings

- Autumn leaves

- Packaging – if you scrunch it up you will adding some temporary structure too

- Shredded paper – but make sure you don't put too much in as it doesn't compact and goes into sludge

- Newspapers – a little at a time; in bulk it is probably best to send them for recycling

All the ingredients in the box above will absorb any liquid, but they can also dry out the compost rather than adding air spaces. It helps to scrunch up paper and card, but this will only provide short-term air spaces, since as soon as the paper or cardboard gets wet it loses its structure (this is why newspapers should be added only a little at a time).

On the other hand, adding only dry plant material leads to a heap that can get too dry. If you feel your heap is too dry, water it – and don't forget that urine is not only wet but a fantastic compost activator!

A bin full of dry hard materials will not decompose.

Mix the peelings with the dry, hard materials and compost happens!

Grass cuttings

It is important to balance out the air-to-water ratio in your compost heap. Fresh grass cuttings are a great way to add water (and heat) to a heap; they are very 'green', full of water and high in nitrogen, so they start to compost very readily. However, they can very quickly become a smelly, sludgy mess. One way of avoiding this is to alternate them with a layer of cardboard. You MUST make the layers of grass cuttings very thin, especially if your grass is lush and well chopped up, or you will create slimy layers. Use a 1" (25mm) layer of grass cuttings and then a layer of flattened-out corrugated cardboard box. Alternatively, mix grass cuttings with more structural material, such as twigs, hedge prunings or woodchip.

Food – the materials you are composting

We know we should eat a balanced diet to be healthy – with proteins, carbohy-drates and plenty of fibre – and the same principle is true of the compost heap, where we want a balance of 'browns' and 'greens' (see page 30).

To add 'food' – sample menus

- Fresh fruit and vegetable peelings with a side order of chips (wood)

- Flattened-out cardboard box with a liberal sprinkling of grass cuttings

- Salad of dandelion leaves tossed with broken-up dry plant stems, etc.

The microbes in the compost heap comprise two main groups: bacteria and fungi. To put it very simply, the bacteria consume the nitrogen and the fungi the carbon. The relationships between not only these two groups of organisms but also all the other microscopic and macroscopic life forms in the compost is incredibly complex – it is an area of research in which much work still needs to be done.

As long as you add a good mixture of materials, balancing wet and dry, with some that will add structure and some that will be absorbent, as well as some fresh green material, and as long as they are mixed well together (so you don't get big air spaces or have denser materials compacted down), then your compost should be fine.

Raw fruit and vegetable peelings are fine to include in any compost heap, but cooked food, meat, fish and dairy products require different treatment. The com-posting of this type of food waste is covered in depth later on in this book. Chapter 4 describes different composting systems and Chapter 9 describes composting food waste on a larger scale, although much of the information in that chapter is relevant whatever scale you are working on. All food waste, cooked or raw, can be com-posted – even fish, meat and dairy products, but these materials are more of a challenge. Firstly, they are very attractive materials for all kinds of creatures, includ-ing rats and flies. Secondly, they can be very smelly, and thirdly, you need to mix them well with other materials for them to compost properly. Cooked food is heavy and dense and needs to have airways provided by structural materials such as woodchip, and also to be mixed with fresh (uncooked) materials to add living bacteria and other microorganisms.

Warmth

The right balance of materials provides the perfect environment for an explosion of microbial populations. Colonies of bacteria can double every hour as long as there is enough warmth.

The most common problem with domestic compost heaps is that, because they are small, they lose heat, and without the heat to drive off moisture they tend to get over-wet, particularly in the colder months of the year.

Because these small 'dalek' bins have no insulation and small cubic capacity they rapidly lose heat, and composting shuts down for the winter.

Maintaining warmth in small heaps/bins, e.g 'daleks'

If you only have space for, or enough materials to fill, a 'dalek' bin, then start composting when the weather has warmed up.

Alternatively, wrap the bin in insulating materials, for example bubble wrap or an old duvet. Sheep's wool is excellent insulation and you can now buy it in sheets and rolls for household insulation. Be aware, however, that the commercially available sheep's wool insulation has polyester in the mix and is not compostable. (One company that can provide pure wool material is Bellacouche, see www.bella-couche.com.) You will need to stitch it or work out a way to hold the insulation up. Some bins, such as the Green Johanna (see page 54), have a fitted 'duvet' as an optional extra.

Maintaining warmth in big heaps/bins

Make the largest heap you can with the materials at hand. Larger heaps have the advantage of being self-insulating, as the outer layer forms an insulating 'jacket' around the central core. A cubic metre is really the minimum for self-insulating heaps; you can contain a heap of this size by using four pallets tied together.

The four stages of making hot compost

Stage one – getting warm

Microorganisms will thrive when you create the ideal conditions. Because bacterial populations can double every hour, within a very short space of time the heap starts to warm up. Different types of bacteria operate at different temperatures. Generally, the hotter the compost gets the faster it breaks down – but even at low temperatures there will be bacteria actively working. The low-temperature bacteria (sychrophiles) give way to warm-temperature bacteria (mesophiles), which operate at 20-30°C.

Many small compost bins never get to the really hot temperatures described below in the next stage, and that's fine as the low- and mid-temperature bacteria and all the other micro and macro organisms will do the job; it will just take a little longer.

Stage two – getting hot

A freshly made heap can get up to 60°C or more within 24 hours. What you have done here is ignite a bacterial bonfire that, as long as there is sufficient moisture and air, will continue to 'burn'. The warm-temperature bacteria are in turn overtaken by the higher-temperature bacteria (thermophiles) and sugar fungi, which operate at 40-70°C. This is seriously hot, and if you have built the heap to keep the air flowing and the heap doesn't choke up, then it will compost rapidly.

This is where a tumbling compost bin (see page 154) is especially useful, because, as long as you have added wood chippings (or something structural), a quick turn will make sure the air reaches all parts of the mass of material.

The advantage of creating high temperatures is that this 'cooks' weed seeds and all the nasty human and plant pathogens in a very short space of time. This is important for commercial composting businesses that need to sell a quality product, and useful for anybody wanting to produce particularly weed-seed-free compost too.

However, don't be concerned if your compost doesn't get to these high temperatures. On a small scale it's more difficult to maintain high temperatures, but a well-made heap in the low-to-mid 40s is pretty hot and over time will do the same work as a high-temperature heap. Hot heaps need turning as much to cool them down as to get more oxygen in; they can actually go up in flames, and even if they don't, prolonged high temperature can result in a product that more closely resembles charcoal than compost. (But don't worry – only very large industrially made compost heaps have the potential to catch fire. Haystacks made from slightly too-damp grass can reach the critical mass that leads to spontaneous combustion. But your 'dalek' bin will not catch fire!) At high temperatures the mid- and low-temperature bacteria just switch off, but they wake up when the temperature drops again. This hot stage of composting can take as little as two weeks, given optimum conditions.

Stage three – cooling down

At this stage the temperature will gradually drop off and no amount of turning will induce the heap to reheat. The heap will be reinvaded by the low- and mid-temperature bacteria and fungi, and this stage will merge almost imperceptibly into the final stage.

This is the time to leave your heap alone – don't turn it anymore. If you have a tumbler, empty the contents into a pile or bin, cover it to stop the rain getting in, and let it quietly mature like a fine wine.

Stage four – maturation

Maturation is the part of composting that cannot be hurried. The chunky woody bits that were so useful at providing airways to help compost the soft, green, wet materials will take a long time to be broken down, primarily by the fungi and creatures such as woodlice that will eat the wood. Worms also move in at this stage and are invaluable, especially at converting the heavier, denser materials into wonderful compost.

Since big chunky woodchip can take years to break down, you can sieve your compost after six months to a year, when you want to harvest it for use (or when you are transferring from a tumbling system into a maturation system, reusing the chunky parts with your new fresh material). Alternatively, do not dig the compost in but use it as a mulch on the surface, where any woody material will not cause 'nitrogen robbery' (see Chapter 6, page 83).

Making cool compost

Of course most of us are adding relatively small amounts at a time to our compost heaps and they don't ever get to really hot temperatures. This is absolutely fine; the lower-temperature bacteria are still working away with all the other micro and macro organisms as long as the temperature is above 6°C. It's important that you mix or layer the green and brown materials (see below) as you go so that you have the magic mantra mix of air and water and your heap will gently, slowly, compost; the worms should invade from below and you will make compost every bit as good as from the hot method – the only small drawback is that any weed seeds will not be cooked.

Browns and greens

Everything you add to the compost heap is primarily composed of carbon (C) and nitrogen (N), plus water (H_2O = hydrogen and oxygen), oxygen (O_2) and other atmospheric gases. The carbon and nitrogen both break down in the compost heap and form a variety of compounds with the oxygen and hydrogen. This chemical process is actually driven by the microscopic organisms that proliferate through the heap – see 'The living soil', below.

Browns – carbon-rich

Materials rich in carbon are also subdivided into:

- **Hard, non-absorbent (or not very absorbent) materials:** e.g. all brown, dead or hard structural parts of plant materials, which provide air. Hard, twiggy materials are not just 'brown' though – just underneath the outer layer of freshly cut prunings and twigs is a thin green cambium layer, where the water is drawn up by the plant. This green part is of course rich in nitrogen and so helps the balance of carbon to nitrogen.

- **Absorbent materials, good at 'mopping up' liquids**, such as paper or cardboard.

The great advantage of the carbon-rich materials is that they are dry and can be stored until you want to blend them with the 'green' materials.

Greens – nitrogen-rich

All fresh green plant material, e.g. grass cuttings, green weeds, vegetable peelings, all food waste (fresh and cooked, meat, fish, dairy, etc. – for more on food waste see Chapters 4 and 9), manures and urine, are high in nitrogen.

If you need extra green materials for your compost you can add nettles and other weeds – however don't do it when they are seeding otherwise you could be sowing weeds for your garden when you spread your compost!

The living soil

Compost builds healthy soils

The pioneers of the organic movement, some of whom were founders of the Soil Association, referred to the soil as 'living'. The prevailing scientific wisdom at the time reduced the soil to a mere mineral substrate, and plant foods were reduced to NPK (nitrogen, phosphorus and potassium), plus lime, magnesium and other mineral supplements. This is still the default position today. We are now realising more and more that the organic pioneers were right: the soil *is* alive.

Unfortunately, soil scientists are now starting to classify some soils as dead. These soils have had decades of chemical applications of fertiliser and pesticides, which kill off the microbial life; they have also been ploughed, using increasingly heavy machinery that 'burns' off the humus and compacts the soil, so driving out all the oxygen.

Plants evolved in soils that had had bacteria and other microscopic organisms in them for millions of years, and they are largely dependent on this complex soil ecosystem.

A gram of healthy soil (roughly a teaspoonful) contains about a billion microscopic organisms: predominantly bacteria (about 600 million) and fungi, comprising literally thousands of different species – around 15,000 species of bacteria per gram and 8,000 species of fungi per gram; actinomycetes, algae and much more. These organisms are called micro flora. There are also micro fauna, which include nematodes (10-100 per gram) and protozoa and rotifers (100,000-1,000,000 per gram).

The above are the main microscopic groups, but in the top 9 inches of healthy soil there are also other larger fauna: mites, springtails, spiders, ants, beetles, centipedes, millipedes, slugs and snails – 10,000-100,000 per square metre – and that's just in the top 9 inches! And then of course there are earthworms – 30-300 per square metre. Now that's a staggering amount of soil life in each gram, in each square metre, and in each acre.

Of course the plants have to fit into this soil space too, and we tend to forget that what we see growing above the ground is really the tip of the iceberg, so to speak. When we rip a weed out of the ground, the visible roots we see are just the structural part of the greater root system, which goes down to the microscopic root hairs. These have formed associations with the bacteria, and it is now estimated that over 80 per cent of plant species have built up symbiotic relationships with mycorrhizal fungi. Legumes are well known for their association with nitrogen-fixing bacteria, and you can see the nodules on their roots.

These symbiotic relationships are still being discovered, but we know that in return for carbohydrates and sugars, which the plant exudes, bacteria and fungi make nitrogen and minerals available to the plant. Various microorganisms also protect the plant from pathogens; they surround the fine root hairs and form a barrier layer that pathogens cannot break through. Mycorrhizal fungi can send out long feeder filaments (hyphae) just a cell thick, seeking out nutrients and minerals far beyond the reach of the plant's roots and bringing them back into the root zone of the plant. The compost heap is the breeding ground for all these microorganisms, which is why organic growers value their compost so highly.

Compost heaps multiply beneficial microorganisms

A well-made compost heap provides the conditions for colonies of bacteria to double every hour, and they soon reach astronomical numbers (a single bacterium can give rise to over eight million bacteria over 24 hours). It is this phenomenal rise in the numbers of bacteria and other microorganisms, all respiring, consuming and reproducing, converting the energy stored in the materials in the heap, which generates the heat.

It's not just the bacteria that multiply in the heap, although the thermophilic (heat-loving) bacteria are the ones that really thrive in these conditions. As the heap cools a whole food web becomes established. When we look into a compost heap we can see only the larger creatures, such as centipedes, woodlice, beetles and worms, but if we get a magnifying glass out a whole host of tiny creatures about the size of a speck of dust are visible – mites, tiny flies and so on. These in turn are feeding on creatures, plant matter and microorganisms out of the range of our sight.

CHAPTER 3

MAKING SUCCESSFUL COMPOST

Gather your materials

Bearing all the advice of the last two chapters in mind, you can build a compost heap or fill a compost bin in one go. It's a most satisfying process – if you can gather together enough of the right materials. For this exercise it's best to avoid cooked food waste, and meat, fish or dairy – see Chapters 4 and 9 for more on dealing with this kind of waste.

- Dry, woody materials. Stockpile wood chippings/shreddings, cardboard, dry plant stems, hay, straw, dry leaves, etc.

- Anything that is fresh and green – if you wait until the spring when every-thing is growing, you can easily find places to cut nettles (which are excellent in the compost heap) and other weeds, as well as grass cuttings.

- All your peelings, etc. from the kitchen; there won't be much of this, which is why it's important to gather nettles and other fresh green sappy growth.

- Any fresh manures you can get to bulk up the heap.

- Garden lime and or wood ash – especially if you have a lot of acidic fruit or coniferous material to compost. Apply only as a thin dusting layer.

Some materials are more or less a perfect balance of browns and greens; for instance, fully unfurled bracken has plenty of wet sappy green growth balanced by the tougher structural stems, and so in theory a pile of bracken can be com-posted on its own. Pea and bean haulms also have just about the perfect balance of browns and greens – dry fibre to lush sappy material (see *Carbon-to-nitrogen ratio* and *Bracken* in the A–Z Guide).

Generally speaking, the more you mix up your material types the better; you cannot necessarily take one 'brown' material and mix it with one 'green' material and end up with perfect compost. Think about what you will need to mix in to add air and absorb moisture. Try to avoid too much of one thing – so, for example, if you prepare masses of squeezed citrus fruit you have a very particular situation to deal with, and will need to think about what will balance not only the nitrogen but also the acidity (see A–Z Guide).

Some individual substances take longer to break down than others, e.g. avocado skins and orange skins, but a few orange skins within a much larger mix of materials are not going to be very significant. I find avocado skins regularly in my finished compost, but they soon break down and disappear when I add that compost to the soil. For more information about specific materials see the A–Z Guide.

Build your heap / fill your bin

It's simple: all you need to do is to create alternating layers of browns and greens. Creating layers is an easy way to mix the two types of material together. You don't *have* to do this – you could mix up the materials in a tumbler or on the ground before piling them into your bin – but layering is probably the easiest way. Just how thick you make each layer very much depends on how wet and dense that material is. For example, fresh lush grass needs to be layered or mixed into the heap as soon as possible with absorbent and/or structural materials. If you leave it to compact and go sludgy and smelly it's very difficult job to get it aerobically composting – go back to the mantra in Chapter 2 if you skipped that bit!

You need a good mix of 'greens' (left) and 'browns' (right).

Filling your compost bin

- Start off with a layer of your coarsest, tougher materials and build up the heap bearing in mind the four-word mantra, particularly remembering the necessary balance between air and water.

- Pay attention to the materials you are layering on to the heap. I find it helps to be continually asking myself, what are the qualities of this forkful? Is it dense, and wet? Has it already started breaking down? Or is it dry and hard? What do I need to put next to this material to help it break down?

- You find you soon get the knack of understanding the needs of the heap, where it will benefit from too-large air spaces being mixed up with denser green materials and where the denser materials need 'fluffing up' and combining with the more structural materials.

- If you find yourself running out of 'greens' then just stop there and save the 'browns' up until you have more fresh materials to add.

- If you find yourself running out of 'browns' then don't be tempted to make a thick layer of dense, wet, green material. You really must find something to mix with it. Cardboard and paper are possibilities that are usually to hand – not ideal on their own without something hard and structural, but OK at a pinch. If you don't mix in the structural materials, however, you will really need to aerate the heap by turning it.

Get the mix right

Too dry?

- If the materials seem too dry you can water the heap – rainwater is best; use a watering can, with a rose or a hose to spread the water evenly. As long as you have plenty of tough, structural materials, which allow excess water to drain away, it's difficult to add too much water.

- The moisture content of a compost heap should be around 50 per cent, but without a moisture meter it's difficult to gauge. However, you start to get a feel for when it's too dry.

- One way to test the dryness of the heap is to take a small amount out, weigh it, pop it into a warm oven overnight and then reweigh it. If it is bone dry and has lost half its weight then you know your heap is half water, which is how it should be. Alternatively, you can just pick up a handful and squeeze – you should only be able to squeeze out a drop or two.

Caution: Do not turn heaps that are musty and dry – give them a thorough soaking first, otherwise you will be releasing all kinds of 'bio-aerosols' such as fungal spores, some of which are not a good idea to inhale (especially **Aspergillus fumigatus,** *which can lead to the condition known as farmer's lung).*

Too wet?

It's most common for compost heaps to be too wet, especially when lots of fresh vegetable peelings, or grass cuttings, etc., are being dumped. These heaps tend to be rather smelly, often with lots of flies. It's best to avoid this situation by always adding structural and absorbent materials to your heap as you go along, rather than trying to rectify the problem afterwards.

- Instead of dumping waste with a high moisture content, mix it with some absorbent or structural materials first, or spread it out in a thin layer to cover the whole surface and then cover this layer with other material. If fruit flies become a problem then you can cover with finished compost, or even with a thin layer of soil.

- If you have serious amounts of citrus fruit, then a sprinkling of garden lime will help too, but the best plan is to mix it with absorbent and structural materials and get it composting as soon as possible.

- Fresh, wet material from the kitchen is high in nitrogen and will quickly become putrescent, so empty your kitchen caddy frequently. Don't leave it to go anaerobic, smelly and attracting flies in your kitchen, especially when the weather is warm – try to empty it daily or at least twice a week. It's more difficult to compost materials once they have started decomposing anaerobically.

- Large amounts of dense, wet material must be opened up as soon as possible with some harder structural materials (such as twigs, tough dry stalks or woodchippings) to allow the air through.

- Cardboard and scrunched-up paper will absorb liquid and add some structure in the short term.

How long does it take?

Compost generally takes six months to a year to fully mature, depending on the time of year you start – it's much faster in warm weather. Turning or tumbling will speed up the first three stages of composting – i.e from warm to hot and back to warm again. There comes a point when turning the compost will not cause it to reheat. It will be 'stabilised' but not fully mature. It then takes several months for the worms to finish off maturing the compost. When it looks like compost (nice and dark), smells like compost (like the woodland litter layer) and feels like compost (sieve a little bit first and it should be like compost out of a bag), then it is compost!

Composting leaves to make leafmould

Before deciduous trees shut down for winter, they extract as much food as they can from their leaves, leaving a carbon-rich autumn leaf to fall. When they land, these leaves are broken down mainly by fungi to become leafmould and provide a marvellous rich source of humus. Leafmould is a really useful material to have for potting and seed-growing media mixes. If you don't have many leaves, just add them to your compost heap.

Leaves can be composted in any simple container that will stop the leaves blowing around. This bin is made from posts and chicken wire.

To make a leafmould bin

To make a simple container that will stop the leaves blowing around, all you need are four posts, set in the ground to form a square, wrapped around with some chicken wire. You don't need a lid or anything fancy. As some leaves take two or more years to break down you might want to build more than one enclosure.

If you have only small amounts of leaves then you could just stuff them into plastic sacks – make sure they are wet when they go in and stab a few holes in the sacks with a fork. Find a place to put these sacks out of the way and the contents will gradually transform over two to three years into leafmould. (NB some leaves, e.g. plane and sycamore leaves, take longer – up to three years.)

Making speedy leafmould

If you have a mower that chops and mixes leaves with the grass you can put both into a bin, which will speed up the composting process. Or you can turn out the leafmould from the bin the following summer, mix it well with fresh lawn mowings and restack. Adding urine to your leafmould will also speed things up!

Sieving your leafmould

Once you've made your leafmould, if you sieve it you get the most wonderful product which you can use as an ingredient in potting and seed composts – see Chapter 6.

CHAPTER 4

CHOOSING THE RIGHT COMPOSTING SYSTEM

How do you choose from the often-bewildering array of composters on the market? Well, it all depends on your situation – whether you live alone or have a large family; whether you live in a flat or have a garden; whether you prepare a lot of food from scratch or have mostly cooked-food leftovers.

There are several different systems that can be used to make compost:

- hot composting – using large or insulated containers

- cool composting – using smaller, uninsulated containers

- Bokashi – which uses a fermentation process

- wormeries – the worms eat the material that you put in

- digesters – which break the material down but you don't have compost to harvest: most of the material breaks down into liquid, which is taken up by the surrounding plants, and much of the rest is pulled into the soil by worms (however, the term 'digester' is actually used to refer to more than one type of system – see page 52).

Some of these systems *can* be part of a two-stage process:

- hot composting is sometimes done in tumblers and then the materials are moved to another container, e.g. a maturation bin, to be matured by worms

- with Bokashi systems you need to bury the materials or add them to a compost heap or wormery to mature.

Anyone with enough space to make compost could compost at least some of their food waste – even if you live in a small flat with no garden it can be done. For example, my sister lives in a flat and has a small wormery on her balcony which she uses for at least some of her peelings and trimmings. (She has to be very careful not to overload it, though, or it can get invaded by fruit flies. Covering the fresh material with a sheet or two of newspaper helps to keep them out.)

Composting systems, boxes and containers broadly fall into two types. The first type deals with fresh, uncooked fruit and vegetable skins and peelings, cardboard and paper, as well as green garden waste materials – prunings, hedge clippings, etc. The second type will deal with all the above but can also be used for other food wastes, such as cooked food, meat, fish, cheese, fats and grease.

See the Resources section for information on suppliers of the different types of composter described in this chapter. Many local authorities provide compost bins at subsidised rates – see www.recyclenow.com/home_composting/buy_a_bin, a website from the Waste and Resources Action Programme, to find out what discounted bins are available in your area.

Systems for uncooked fruit and vegetable peelings, cardboard, paper and green garden waste

Dalek bin

The compost bin that most people are familiar with is the plastic 'dalek'-type bin, promoted by many local authorities. Sizes vary from just over 200 litres to 350 litres, some have access/inspection hatches, and they come in a variety of colours. Millions of these are now in use in the UK. There are also flat-sided, square or rectangular bins. The smaller ones have a cubic capacity equivalent to the dalek bins and are used in exactly the same way.

Don't be put off by the rather long list of 'cons' below. If you don't have much space these bins are a great solution and can be easily moved around the garden. You can hide them amongst tall plants or in a border and move them regularly – after moving it you will find the most wonderful soil where the dalek has been sitting.

As long as you get the mix right as you fill the bin you will be able to make good compost for most of the year, although in the depths of winter it will slow right down or stop unless you insulate it really well.

Plastic bins also come in square or other shapes. These often tend to be larger than the daleks and come with base plates, in which case they can be used for composting all types of food waste – see page 62.

How it works
Daleks are lightweight, so you can move them around the garden easily and plonk them down where you want either on earth or hard ground. They contain your materials, so you just need to mix or layer the materials as they go in.

A common 'dalek' bin design includes a hatch for accessing the finished product.

When they are getting pretty full, lift the whole bin up – as if making a sandcastle – and if you have enough space put the bin down next to your compost castle and fork the top, uncomposted layers back into the bin. The bottom section should be nicely composted and ready to use. Alternatively you can bag it up for when you need it.

Cost

There are many different companies offering these kinds of bins, and prices will vary according to make and size. Some councils have given bins away free; other councils pass on the benefits of being able to bulk-buy, so that the bins are offered at wholesale cost price, often around £12-15. If you buy at full retail price at a garden centre or through a mail-order company you can expect to pay double this and even more for some of the larger models.

Emptying Dalek bins without hatches could be viewed as a pro and a con, in that you have to lift up the whole bin – but because of its shape this is very easy, unless plant growth around the base has fused it to the ground. If this is the case it's still pretty easy to go around with a spade and free it all up first. Then you can access the whole pile of material and scoop the top off ready to be further composted.

Where to get one

Many local authorities provide daleks at subsidised rates – see www.recyclenow. com/home_composting/buy_a_bin to find out what offers are available in your area. Most garden centres, garden catalogues and online retailers will have a selection, or you can order direct from the manufacturer.

Pros of daleks

- Cheap; have been given away by councils free!
- Easy to install – just plonk down anywhere. They can be used on the bare ground, on grass or hard standing.
- Good for small gardens.

Cons of daleks

- The generally small size means they cannot maintain heat and so composting takes longer.
- The lack of base means that unwanted furry creatures can get in easily (although you can set the bins up on hard standing, paving slabs, etc. and put wire mesh down and bend it around the bin to stop them).
- Emptying (see below). The ones with a hatch tend not to behave in the way the manufacturer's glossy brochure would have you believe – i.e. a lovely cascade of peat-like substance practically harvesting itself through the hatch.
- Trying to shovel material out through the hatch often results in you bashing and damaging the sides of the bin, and as the composter ages and goes brittle the hatch door finally stops working.

New Zealand box

These boxes can be bought or made and are generally of generous proportions, each box being around a cubic metre and often bigger. They are usually made of wood and have a front made of planks, which slide up and off to access the compost when needed.

They can be single compartments but are more often constructed in series of two or more, so that heaps can be turned from one compartment into the next. Some have lids, or you can buy duvet-type covers for them to help keep them warm, or use old carpet cut to size. They can be lined with mesh to keep out rats and are a popular choice for garden composting.

A pair of New Zealand boxes.

How it works

Because a New Zealand box has a large surface area and is easily accessible you can add alternate layers of greens and browns without difficulty. Worms living in the layer underneath the most recent deposits generally rapidly invade these heaps, unless of course you have assembled a large pile in one go and it is hot.

Cost

A New Zealand box is free if you make your own from scrap materials (also see home-made bin, page 48). Otherwise they cost from £80 for a manufactured single chamber bin to over £200 for a triple bin.

Pros of New Zealand boxes

- Can be home-made or bought ready-made.
- Easily accessible for adding material to.
- Good size.
- User-friendly and great for dealing with larger volumes and bulky materials.
- Easy to turn if you have more than one bin.

Cons of New Zealand boxes

- Wooden ones will rot eventually.
- Needs cover on top and wire underneath to make it vermin-proof.

Where to get one

Garden centres, gardening catalogues and online retailers.

Wooden slatted composter

This is essentially the same design as a New Zealand box; it is made from identical planks with two slots in each end that you put together to construct a cube, either solid or slatted. The difference is that a New Zealand Box has a removable front, whereas with these bins you need to deconstruct all four sides to get all the material out.

Cost

£35 to £80.

Pros of wooden slatted composters

- Reasonably quick and easy to assemble.
- Easy to transport.
- Good size.

Cons of wooden slatted composters

- You have to deconstruct the whole bin to get to the bottom.
- If the sides are slatted the outside tends to dry out too much.

Where to get one
Garden centres, gardening catalogues and online retailers.

Beehive composter

These compost bins look really nice, which is their main selling point, and they come in a range of tasteful colours, natural wood or plastic lumber. Each section lifts off, making emptying very easy, and there is usually a hatch at the bottom as well. The bins work the same way as any small garden composter, e.g. a dalek bin.

Cost
£90 to £160.

Pros of beehive composters

- Looks – you don't need to hide your compost heap!
- Range of colours.
- Easy to empty.

Cons of beehive composters

- Rather expensive – you pay for the look.

Where to get one
Garden centres, gardening catalogues and online retailers.

Vertical composting unit

There's only one bin I know of that uses gravity on a domestic level and that is the 'Earthmaker', invented in New Zealand. It has a generous capacity and a unique design; the three chambers have a total capacity of 466 litres and the bin stands 1.2 metres tall with a diameter of 75cm.

How it works

The bin has three chambers inside. When the top chamber is filled then the floor of that compartment is pulled out, allowing the material to fall down a slide in the next chamber and so on down to the final chamber at the base. This means that when the material is held in the top compartment it is more inaccessible to rodents, and then instead of you having to turn the material the composter uses gravity to do the hard work by tumbling the material down slopes into the lower compartments.

Cost

£140.

The Earthmaker bin has three chambers, allowing gravity to do the hard work of tumbling the compost.

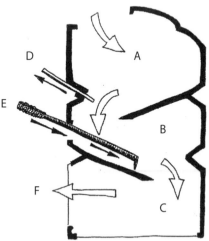

A Top chamber – adding and mixing
B Middle chamber
C Maturation chamber
D Slide pulls out to allow material to drop into the lower chambers
E Tool to push material down slope
F Harvesting when door removed

Pros of vertical composting units

- Takes the hard work out of turning.

- Holding the fresh material at the top takes this often-enticing material away from the easy access of rats.

- Generous size.

Cons of vertical composting units

- Mixed messages from the manufacturer about what types of food waste you can compost: some parts of the instructions say put in cooked food waste, etc.; other parts say don't.

- Access to the material inside the bin – I found the harpoon provided and the hole you have to push it through very annoying!

Where to get one

Earthmaker (www.earthmaker.co.uk), garden centres, gardening catalogues and online retailers.

Home-made bin

All kinds of things can be adapted to contain materials for composting.

- Stout wire mesh, such as pig netting, can be made into a cylinder and lined with old carpet, which you can roughly sew through to attach to the wire frame.

- Old doors, corrugated iron sheeting and all manner of discarded panels can be used to make simple containers.

- You can construct bins from concrete blocks and make a front section of sliding wooden planks.

- One of the best containers I ever made was made from hay bales – lovely and insulating. I covered that one with corrugated iron and more bales in the winter, and it worked a treat.

- The simplest compost heap of all is just a pile on the ground covered with a tarpaulin or old carpet.

- Or you could make a beautiful one and copy the beehive compost design (see page 46).

When you construct your bin, make sure that air can flow through it and liquids can drain out, or you will be creating an anaerobic alcohol-producing still!

I use two pallet bins for general rough allotment and garden stuff, and I fill a third one with sawdust and shavings to part-rot down for my 'humanure' system (see the A–Z Guide).

Cost
Free – or the cost of the materials.

Pros of home-made bins

- Cheap or free.
- Fun to make.

Cons of home-made bins

- Difficult to vermin-proof completely.
- Can be a bit unsightly or very lovely, depending on your DIY skills!
- You need to make sure to avoid potentially toxic materials in their construction.

How to construct a simple box-type compost bin without sliding front panels

- Get hold of some pallets and tie them together – I use baler twine, which is freely available where I live and very strong. Because pallets are double-layered they stand up easily too.
- If you want you can fill the gaps in the pallets with more wood or attach cardboard sheets to the inside to stop matter falling between the gaps and to help insulate the bin. The cardboard will rot eventually but should do its job in the meantime. You can also use plastic sheeting, which helps keep moisture in.
- You can make a rat-proof bin by nailing weldmesh to each pallet, but it is difficult to get a neat-fitting lid to exclude them entirely.

Top left and right: pallets make great compost containers and can either just be tied to each other or supported by poles. Centre left: compost reduces dramatically as the ingredients break down. Centre right: the sawdust pile pictured below after 6-8 months and applications of urine and water.

Windrows

How they work

Of course you don't actually need a bin at all. Larger amounts of materials are probably best composted in elongated piles called 'windrows' (pictured overleaf). If you have several cubic metres of material to compost then this is a good method. You can make the piles as large as you like, bearing in mind that denser materials will compact down more the higher you build. You build a pile and add more to one side and continue to build and extend sideways as long as you have materials and space to do so. The pile is wider at the base, slopes in as it is built up and usually has a flat top. Windrows can either be covered with a kind of thatch of grass, hay or straw, etc. or can be covered with a sheet of plastic or a tarpaulin. Biodynamic compost is generally made this way, and this method is best for large amounts of woody material (see the A–Z Guide for both of these).

Cost

Free.

Pros of windrows

- No construction materials whatsoever.

- You can make the piles as large as you like.

- Fits perfectly with the biodynamic ethos.

- This system can also be used with specialised machinery – windrow turners can be attached to tractors for large-scale operations, or may even be stand-alone machines.

- Really good for heavy dense materials, such as manures, when used with machinery to turn them.

- Very high long-term windrows can also work for woody materials.

Cons of windrows

- You need a lot of materials to construct a pile.

- This takes time and care to make neatly – you need skill to get the mix right.

- Large machinery systems need level hard standing to work effectively.

Large amounts of material can be layered and stacked into elongated piles called windrows. These ones are from a biodynamic garden.

Systems for any food waste, including cooked food, meat, fish, dairy products, etc.

Cooked food waste and meat, fish and dairy is the most problematic material to compost because it is dense, heavy, wet and smelly and it attracts unwanted visitors such as rats and flies. Many different systems and strategies have been developed to deal with this type of waste. These fall broadly into two types.

1. Aerobic sealed systems

- 'In-vessel' systems – sealed containers that rats cannot get into but which generally have some sort of air and liquid flow systems built in. 'In vessel' generally refers to large-scale systems, as described in Chapter 9, but really the term applies to any small sealed systems, such as tumbling bins or even compost bins such as the Green Johanna (see page 54).

2. Anaerobic sealed systems

- Digesters – this generally refers to 'anaerobic' (without air) digestion – which is the subject of another book entirely! The digester referred to opposite, the Green Cone, is really misdescribed by this term, but that is how the company that makes it describes it.

- Fermenters – this is also a type of anaerobic system. It uses anaerobic microorganisms that stop the food waste from smelling disgusting and ferment it in the same way you might make sauerkraut.

Remember that any heavy, dense wet materials, which includes this type of food waste, need to have structural materials added to create airways.

Green Cone (digester)

The only 'digester' I know of on the market is the Green Cone. 'Digestion' is generally a term used to describe decomposition without air, i.e. 'anaerobic digestion', but Green Cone describes its product as a digester – I guess because it is not really composting. You don't mix your kitchen waste with structural or absorbent materials. The Green Cone consists of a basket, rather like a washing basket, which is buried in the ground and forms the base for a double-skin cone above the ground: a design that makes it difficult for rats to get in.

How it works

A Green Cone digester is more of a waste-disposal option, since you don't harvest the compost. The material breaks down and is pulled into the surrounding soil by worms. Since kitchen waste is largely liquid, much of this also goes into the soil, where the nearby plants can take it up.

Green Cones have to be installed carefully: try to install them on level ground as it's important that the basket is completely underground. (I've seen them on fairly steep slopes where part of the basket was exposed). Soil is a great deodoriser and so it's important that the soil completely surrounds the cone. If you are on clay soil then you will have to dig out a bigger hole and put some coarse drainage, such as stones or bricks, in the bottom.

The Green Cone: only half of the composter is visible above ground.

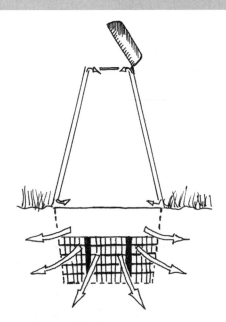

Unless you are very frugal in their use, Green Cones will need moving after a year or two, depending on your soil type and how much you put in them. You can line the basket with wire mesh if you want to be completely sure of rats not getting in (though I don't think even wire mesh would stop the badgers!).

Cost

£75. (Check out www.recyclenow.com/home_composting/buy_a_bin to see if your council is offering them at a discounted price.)

Pros of Green Cones

- Can take all kinds of food waste, including both cooked and raw.
- It's a bit like an iceberg in that most of it is beneath the surface – so the small cone above ground can be hidden among tall plants in a flower border, for example.

Cons of Green Cones

- You don't get any compost out of it!
- You will have to move it at some stage.
- They are not totally rat (or badger) proof – I know plenty of people who really swear by them and others that don't like them, which just shows that it's important to try to get the system that suits your situation. One National Trust property I visited had a whole area devoted to them and, apart from the badger getting in, they were working fine.

Where to get one

Green Cones are available directly from Green Cone (www.greencone.com), and also through some councils and some garden centres, as well as online retailers.

Green Johanna composter

How it works

Green Johannas are bigger than most dalek-type bins (95cm tall and 90cm wide at the base). They are fully sealed with a perforated base plate so that rats cannot get in but worms can. The great advantage of this system is that you can put anything in – you don't have to separate out kitchen waste, cooked or raw, from garden waste as they are rat- and mouse-resistant. You still want to mix structural and absorbent materials in, as this is an aerobic composting system. Green Johannas come with a range of extra accessories (at a price), including a 'duvet' to keep your compost warm and active in the winter – which really helps to insulate your compost during the cold months.

Cost

£114 (or £139 with a winter duvet jacket).

The Green Johanna is larger than most dalek bins, and fully sealed.

Where to get one

Available from Green Cone (www.greencone.com), as well as online retailers.

> #### Pros of Green Johannas
>
> - They can take anything.
> - Their size means they hold heat more efficiently – and the duvet means you can keep them going through the colder months.
>
> #### Cons of Green Johannas
>
> - Cost of bin and extra cost for duvet, if wanted.
> - Emptying could be a slight concern as it's through a hatch.
> - You need a bit more space to site it than for a normal dalek bin.

Bokashi

The Effective Microorganism ('EM') Bokashi system is an airless fermentation system that uses a special selection of bacteria, fungi and actinomycetes (micro-

You can keep your Bokashi bins in the kitchen, as the container also serves as a caddy.

scopic organisms that suppress harmful bacteria and fungi), which thrive without air to ferment the material. Unlike most airless systems, Bokashi does this without unpleasant smells, and can be placed and used within the kitchen or some other warm part of your house or flat. (Many foods are preserved using fermentation processes, such as yoghurt, sourdough bread, beer and sauerkraut.)

Bokashi is particularly useful as a 'first stage' for food waste (you then need to bury it or add it to a normal compost heap) as it will take any food waste – cooked, raw, meat, fish and dairy can all go into a Bokashi system.

How it works

There are two pairs of buckets. Each pair fits together – the one on top has holes drilled in the bottom, so that liquids can collect in the second bucket underneath. You can scale this system up – I have heard of wheelie bins being used as containers.

The kit also includes a bag of Bokashi mix, which is a combination of bran and microorganisms.

Pros of the Bokashi system

- You can ferment any food waste in the system and then either bury it in the garden or add it to any compost heap, e.g. a dalek, and it will not attract rats and flies.

- The small size and the fact that you have to compact the materials down means you can even have the system fermenting in your kitchen.

- Cheap – you can make your own system using nesting plastic containers with snap-on lids – like large ice cream containers, which you can usually get hold of from places selling, er, ice cream!

- The Bokashi system is used with great success by some community groups collecting food waste on housing estates in London, as a way of stopping rats, foxes, flies and other insects being attracted by the smell of rotting food (see Chapters 7 and 9).

Cons of the Bokashi system

- If you buy a system you will pay quite a lot of money for four buckets; however, you can make your own for free.

- You have to buy the Bokashi microorganisms mix.

- You will need open ground or a compost heap to bury the fermented Bokashi.

- Smell – a few people don't like the smell, but it is very mild and nothing like the awful stink you can get from putrefying food waste. Most people find it completely inoffensive.

Every time you add material (e.g. chopped-up food scraps) to the top bucket, you add a little sprinkling of the Bokashi mix, push the material down firmly to squeeze out any liquids and remove as much air as possible, and re-seal the lid.

When the top bucket is full, you start using the second set of buckets. When the second set is full, empty the first set and use that again. The first bucket should have been left sealed for about two weeks, or you can leave it for longer. If you need to fill buckets more quickly than this, then you can either use more buckets or use larger ones.

The liquid that gathers in the bottom bucket can also be diluted and used as a wonderful organic liquid fertiliser for your houseplants and garden plants.

Cost

Systems start at £20 for a simple pair of buckets and packet of EM bran, and go up to £60 for larger, more sophisticated buckets – the EM impregnated bran costs about £5 for a 600g bag, depending on the supplier. You can easily make your own bucket sets from freely available large ice cream containers and just buy the bran.

Where to get one

Living Soil (www.livingsoil.co.uk). For more information on EM Bokashi, see Effective Microorganisms Ltd (www.effectivemicro-organisms.co.uk).

Wormery

Small amounts of any food waste, whether raw or cooked, can be added to wormeries. Worms can eat only relatively small amounts at a time, and if you add too much the wormery is likely to heat up or attract flies. See Chapter 5 for full details of this type of system.

Burying food waste (cooked and raw food)

How it works

Many gardeners bury kitchen scraps in a trench, particularly in the winter; this then becomes a site for their runner beans or other legumes in the following season. However, don't do this with woody materials, as it causes 'nitrogen robbery' (i.e. it takes the nitrogen away from the growing plants).

Cost

Free.

Pros of burying food waste

- Simple and free.

Cons of burying food waste

- You need to have the space.

- You can have foxes, badgers or rats visiting and digging it all up! I think it was a badger that destroyed my attempts to do this.

Tumbler

How it works

There are many different sorts of tumbling bins on the market now. Some are drums that flip end over end; the larger ones revolve around a central axle mounted on a stand, or sit on a base unit with rollers; and there are even 'compost spheres', which you can roll around the lawn (see opposite).

Tumbling your compost speeds up the composting process by adding air. However, you have to be careful you don't overdo the tumbling, which can result in the materials drying out too much. Just give it a good tumble every day or whenever you put more stuff in.

This process of aeration is good for uncooked fruit and vegetable waste because they are dense and wet. But you must still add some coarse woody material such as woodchip, otherwise your tumbler could become more like a dough-making machine!

Cost

Small 'end over end' types and compost spheres start at £95. Larger ones can range from £170 to £900 (see Chapter 9 for more on these top-of-the-range, insulated tumblers).

A simple, uninsulated, end-over-end tumbler.

Pros of tumblers

- Makes the job of turning your compost very easy.

- Compost is secure and sealed in the vessel, which means that rats, mice and most flies, etc. cannot get in, so it's great for all food waste.

- Accelerates the composting process – especially the volatile hot first phase (see Chapter 2).

- Tumblers are also useful for dealing with perennial weeds, and for mixing materials. The compost they produce can be used directly on the garden as long as it is well composted. I prefer to put the compost from my tumbler into a maturation bin, allowing worms to finish it off.

Cons of tumblers

- Expensive.

- Can get very heavy and difficult to turn.

- They take up quite a bit of space.

- You need a supply of (ideally dry) woodchip to mix with the food waste.

- Prone to attract small fruit flies if you don't get the mix right and maintain high temperatures.

Where to get one
Tumblers are available through large garden centres, gardening catalogues and online retailers.

CompoSphere

This is a type of tumbler (see left) that you can roll around the garden to aerate your compost.

Cost
£75 to £97.

Where to get one
Available from online retailers.

Square and other shaped bins

Larger flat-sided bins are also available and come with (sometimes optional) bases. If used with the base then they can be suitable for composting all types of food waste. The best ones are made of thicker insulating plastic: examples are the Eco King and Thermo King, with 400-litre, 600-litre and 900-litre models available. If you use the base plates then the bins can be used in the same way as the Scotty's Hot Box, although the smaller sizes will not have the same self-insulation properties. (NB if you use them without the base plate it is not recommended you use them for food waste). Scotty's Hot Box (see below) is 1,000 cubic litres or a cubic metre, and has an impermeable base.

Cost
The 400-litre models cost around £60, the 600-litre £80 and the 900-litre £100.

Where to get one
Online retailers, such as Green Fingers.

Scotty's Hot Box

The Scotty's Hot Box was not designed for householders but as a secure matura-tion box to take larger amounts of food waste from tumblers or other food waste systems, e.g. larger systems in schools, etc. However, some householders do use it as it is a good general-purpose composter too – the generous size and insulation means you can get hot compost and you can even mix in a certain amount of cooked food waste and meat, fish or dairy as long as you make sure it is well mixed with plenty of garden materials in an actively hot composting state. See Chapter 9, page 164, for details of the Scotty's Hot Box.

Choosing the system that suits your space

The table opposite summarises the types of composter that would be suitable for all different situations – from a flat with no outside space to a large garden that will generate a lot of green material.

Many people I talk to think that you have to place a compost bin directly on the soil to allow the worms in. In fact, however, you can make compost in containers raised off the ground or on concrete – worms have a remarkable way of finding compost bins, wherever you put them. The exception is the Green Cone, which needs to be dug into the ground so is not suitable if you have only a concreted area or patio.

Quick guide to space needed for composting systems						
	No outside space*	Balcony only*	Small shared outside space	Large shared outside space	Small garden	Large garden
Bokashi	✓	✓	✓	✓	✓	✓
Wormery	✓	✓	✓	✓	✓	✓
Earthmaker			✓	✓	✓	✓
Dalek			✓	✓	✓	✓
Green Cone			✓	✓	✓	✓
Green Johanna			✓	✓	✓	✓
Tumbler			✓	✓	✓	✓
In-vessel				✓	✓	✓
New Zealand box				✓	✓	✓
Heaps (small windrows)				✓	✓	✓
Leafmould				✓	✓	✓
Scotty's Hot Box				✓		✓
Community scheme	✓	✓	✓	✓	✓	✓
Windrows				✓		✓

* If you have only a balcony, or no outside space at all, you will probably not be able to deal with all of your compostables – it will depend on how much fresh food you eat, as this generates quantities of peelings, and how careful you are not to have any wasted food to dispose of. You could use just a wormery or a Bokashi and a wormery. Be very careful about putting lots of fruit peel in a wormery, otherwise you could be invaded by fruit flies – a Bokashi system coupled with a wormery may be your best bet, although you will still not want to dump the entire contents of a Bokashi bucket on your worms in one dollop. You can add more Bokashi compost at one time to a wormery than if it was fresh material, but try to space it out over a few days – the fermenting material with the Bokashi mix will keep fine in its sealed container.

If you have no outside space at all you have the most challenging composting situation: I have heard of people keeping worms in a window seat, and you certainly can keep worms inside, but always leave a low-wattage light on in the room at night or you will find they tend to wander! However, this approach is really only for the real enthusiast prepared to put up with the almost inevitable fruit flies at some time.

How much material do you have and of what sort?

As explained in Chapter 2, there are two main categories of materials for composting: 'browns' and 'greens'.

And there are two main sources of materials:

- the garden – these materials are generally unattractive to rodents

- the kitchen – these materials are a mix of 'safe' (not very attractive as food for rodents, e.g fruit peel, onion skins, tea leaves, coffee grounds) and 'unsafe' attractant materials, e.g. cooked food, dairy products, meat and fish.

You *could* divide the materials from your kitchen into two categories – one to go in a garden system (Box 1, below) and one to go in one of the systems in Box 2, page 66. However, in practice and for a better composting mix you might find it easier to just mix *all* the materials from your kitchen and put them into one of the systems in Box 2.

   The two boxes on the following pages show how you can separate out the materials and give an idea of the amounts you will be able to handle through each type of system. The first box relates to dry, hard, carbon-rich materials and soft, green materials, and the second box relates to food waste, both raw and cooked.

Box 1

How to use dry, hard, carbon-rich material

You can safely leave this in a pile to gently rot down and use as needed, or store to mix or layer with nitrogen-rich (green) materials. These materials can be composted in any amounts, sometimes on their own, or mixed as described below.

Large-diameter woody materials

Dry them to use as firewood or to build wildlife refuge piles in the garden.

Woody brash, shredded (branches, etc.)

- Put straight on the garden – mulch for paths or perennials, or on top of barrier mulch (see page 86), e.g. cardboard or paper.

(cont'd opposite)

- Leave for long-term slow breakdown for use when needed:

  > mixed roughly 50:50 with soft, high-nitrogen garden materials (e.g. grass cuttings) in any garden composting system

  > mixed with food waste roughly 50:50 (raw and cooked) in an enclosed system, e.g. a Green Johanna, tumbler or other in-vessel system

  > rotted down and use as a 'soak' with humanure systems (see A–Z Guide).

Woody brash, unshredded (branches, etc.)

- Make long-term woody piles – stacked as tightly and as high as possible for long, slow breakdown – eventually, after two to three years, pull apart and sieve. In the meantime the pile will act as wildlife habitat.

- Chop up or saw and dry for kindling.

- Use poles and sticks for plant supports for peas and beans, etc.

If you don't have a shredder but have a lot of large woody material then it may be best to take it to a local community composting scheme (see Chapter 7) if there is one nearby, or your local authority may collect it or have a site you can take it to. If you have enough space you can find a quiet corner to stack it as neatly and as high as possible and let it become a wonderful wildlife resource.

Other dry, hard, woody materials (prunings, dry plant stems, etc.)

- Shred and use exactly as shredded brash, above.

- Mix or layer roughly 50:50 with soft garden clippings, grass cuttings, weeds, etc., in a garden compost system.

- Mix roughly 50:50 with food waste (raw and cooked) in an enclosed system, such as a Green Johanna, tumbler or other in-vessel system.

Paper and cardboard

- Add to garden composting systems as an absorbent material – i.e. layer with grass cuttings or soft green weeds (again, roughly 50:50 but best mixed with some structural woody material as well).

(cont'd overleaf)

- Use to line the kitchen caddy. Some scrunched-up paper or cardboard in the caddy is useful to absorb juices.

- Put straight on the garden as a 'barrier' in a barrier mulch system (see 'Woody brash – shredded', pages 64-5).

How to use soft green materials

'Soft green materials' include raw fruit and vegetables from the kitchen, and weeds and grass cuttings from the garden. These are all best mixed or layered with absorbent and structural materials straight away, in a garden compost system, as described above.

Box 2

How to compost all food waste from your kitchen

Cooked food, dairy products, meat and fish need to be incorporated into a compost system straight away.

Wormery

You can add only small amounts at a time to a wormery – fresh, raw material will heat up if too much is added at a time. Spread it out in a thin layer over the surface. The worms can eat it only when it starts to decompose. See Chapter 5 for more about wormeries.

Bokashi

- As long as you layer the waste with the Bokashi mix (see page 56) and squash out as much air as possible, you can either fill any size of container in one go or, as the food waste arises, add it to the container until it is full.

- When you have filled your second Bokashi container, empty the first (as long as the material has been in there for at least ten days) into your garden compost system or wormery, or bury the material.

Green Cone (digester)

These are designed for household use, and a normal amount of household food waste should easily fit in one. Larger quantities will need more than one digester, or you could use a different system, e.g. a tumbler.

(cont'd opposite)

Green Johanna

- Mix the food waste 50:50 with woody materials, as described in Box 1.

- When the bin is full you can start trying to harvest from the hatch. If it's not ready, because you need to process a lot of material, you will need another Green Johanna or need to consider a larger system (e.g. the Scotty's Hot Box or a faster system, such as the Jora 270 tumbler – see Chapter 9).

Tumbler

- Mix 50:50 with woody materials, as described in Box 1. When the tumbler is getting full you can either:

  > stop adding food waste (in which case you will need to use another system as well or you will have material going to waste in your dustbin)

  > empty the material from the tumbler into a maturation bin (i.e. a two-step composting process).

- Some tumblers (e.g. the Jora 270) have double compartments which enable you to finish the composting process in one side while adding fresh material to the other side.

- If you have too much material for a tumbler then you need to look at larger systems – see Chapter 9.

CHAPTER 5
COMPOSTING WITH WORMS

Worms are a natural part of the composting process, invading heaps after all the heat and excitement generated during the hot phase of composting, which also releases masses of liquid from the decomposing materials. The worms that colonise compost heaps are native species, which live on the surface, in the litter layer of the soil. In a compost heap they feed away immediately under the fresh layer of waste, and so the larger the surface area in a wormery the better. However, the wormeries on the market tend to be fairly vertical in shape, which makes them more convenient to fit into small spaces, but remember it is the surface area that limits how much you can add at any one time.

Whenever I take my portable wormery into a school it always generates huge enthusiasm from the staff and children alike. Some people really can't stand the worms but most are fascinated by them. I love them for creating the very best compost and also for showing me that I've got the right conditions for them to thrive. When I take the front panels off one of my bins I expect to see a veritable waterfall of worms. I generally use them to finish the compost coming from my

'Worm city' – a wormery demonstration area at Spitalfields City Farm, London.

hot tumbling systems as, sadly, it is all too easy to kill off worms by overloading them with material. Nevertheless, many people use wormeries as 'one-stop shops' to process material from start to finish. If you do use a wormery as a 'one stop shop' in this way, do be prepared for more problems with flies, especially fruit flies, and for the liquid released as the fresh material breaks down.

Pros of composting with worms

- Will deal with any kind of food waste.
- Makes the best, richest compost.
- Provides you with liquid feed.
- Fun! Kids love them too.
- Can fit into a small space.
- It's a great way to finish off the compost from a tumbler system.

Cons of composting with worms

- Worms can eat only a small amount at a time.
- Adding too much material at once can cause the contents to heat up too much, which the worms don't like, and could result in dead worms.
- The wormery will start to fill up with leachate if it is not regularly tapped off – and if the tap blocks up the worms will all die (and it will smell really bad!).
- If you add too much fruit you will attract fruit flies – it helps if you can bury the fruit just under the surface.
- If you add any fresh meat you will attract blowflies – but, as with fruit, you can bury small amounts.

Types of wormery

The majority of wormeries are made out of plastic. There are three types.

1. A single container – some resemble small wheelie bins with a tap at the bottom. Inside at the base is a perforated layer, which allows liquid through.

2. A stacking system of shallow boxes with perforated bases – these systems are more expensive but make the emptying easier.

3. A worm bag: sold by The Worm Research Centre, a 'worm bag' is a woven polypropylene bag that is breathable, allowing air and liquids through but not flies. It sits inside a container like a small wheelie bin or dustbin.

If you know nothing about wormeries, consider buying your wormery complete with a starter kit – this will contain all you need:

*   instructions
*   worms
*   bedding
*   ground limestone
*   sometimes, worm treats and moisture mats.

Your local council may be offering a specific type of wormery at a reduced price, or you can easily research types and sources from many websites (see Resources section).

Single-container wormery

These generally resemble a small wheelie bin. Some have an insulated jacket, which is a really good extra to get. They have a tap on the bottom to collect the liquid.

Pros of single-container wormeries

*   Upright shape: it fits into a small space.
*   Everything you need is included.
*   Can deal with all kitchen waste.

Cons of single-container wormeries

*   Small surface area limits the area the worms can work.
*   Can deal with only small quantities per day.
*   Taps get clogged easily and worms drown as a result.
*   Whole container needs to be emptied when it is time to harvest the worm casts.

Cost
From £50, including everything you need – worms, bedding, etc.

Where to get one
Available from garden centres and online retailers.

Stacking-system wormery

This is a nesting stack of round or rectangular containers on a base unit, which has a tap.

Pros of stacking wormeries

- Makes emptying much easier – the worms migrate upwards as the wormery is filled, and when all the trays are full you simply remove the lowest tray, empty it and it becomes the new top tray.
- All the other pros of the single-container composting system apply.

Cons of stacking composters

- Small surface area limits the area the worms can work.
- Can deal with only small quantities per day.
- Taps get clogged easily and worms drown as a result.
- Whole container needs to be emptied when it is time to harvest the worm casts.
- Extra cost.

Cost
From £87, including everything you need – worms, bedding, etc.

Where to get one
Available from garden centres and online retailers.

Worm Bag

This is pretty much the same as the single container except that the worms, bedding and all the materials go into a woven polypropelene bag inside the external container.

Cost
£25.

Where to get one
Available from The Worm Research Centre (www.wormresearchcentre.co.uk).

Pros of worm bags

- The advantage of this is that it excludes fruit flies, which can sometimes be a nuisance with wormeries. (You could incorporate this feature into a home-made wormery).
- To empty you can lift the whole bag out.

Cons of worm bags

- Suitable only for fairly small containers.
- You have to undo a clip on the bag every time you want to put anything in the wormery.

Making your own wormery

Once you start keeping worms you will almost certainly want to increase your capacity – the more worms and wormeries you have, the more material you can process. Worms take their time and so, rather than forking out money buying lots of commercial wormeries, why not make your own?

Wormeries are so simple to make even I can do it! You can often find suitable containers for free or very cheaply; for instance I was given a plastic barrel with a split in it, making it useless for holding water but ideal to convert into a wormery.

Cost

Home-made systems can be free if made from found or scrap items and worms taken from a compost heap or manure pile; otherwise expect to pay from £45 to £100 (See Resources for some suppliers of worms).

Containers

If you are making a home for any animal, you have to provide a suitable living environment. Many large containers (such as old dustbins and barrels) can be adapted for making your own wormery. I have several wormery containers; my best ones are old degassed chest freezers, which keep the worms warm in winter and cool in summer. The following are some suggestions; for more ideas on making your own wormery see www.wikihow.com/Make-Your-Own-Worm-Compost-System.

Compost in progress

'Greens' – vegetable scraps

'Browns' – cardboard and dry plant material

Autumn leaves will break down in a year or two to make lovely leafmould

Woody garden waste makes great refuges for wildlife

Community composting in action with Chudleigh Rotters

Compost ready to use

Composting food waste at school using a Jora 270 tumbler

Building a New Zealand box

Stinging nettle – a compost activator

Comfrey – stuff it into a barrel to make liquid feed

The Green Cone – most of the composting goes on below ground

A standard dalek and a Rotol dalek bin (front)

Compost in raised beds ready for planting

Stacking wormery

You can make your own stacking wormery by adapting nesting or stacking plastic containers, as illustrated below. These can be large rectangular storage containers, similar to the boxes used by councils for recycling, or smaller containers – two or three of these will make a good system.

- Find three square or rectangular containers the same size, with a lid for the top one.

- Drill plenty of holes of at least half a centimetre diameter in the bottom of two of the containers; the third will be the base container.

- Drill lots of small holes in the lid (as small as possible to allow air in but ideally keep fruit flies out – about the size of these bullet points).

- The liquids need to be able to drain away from the worms' bedding layer in the base container. You can either a) drill holes in the bottom of the base container and set up the finished wormery on blocks – if you then want to harvest any liquid you will also need to put a piece of plastic sheet underneath

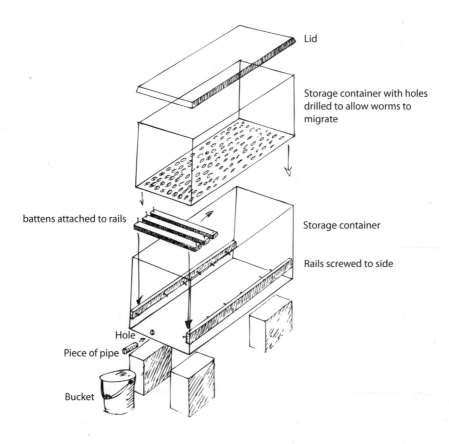

Lid

Storage container with holes drilled to allow worms to migrate

battens attached to rails

Storage container

Rails screwed to side

Hole

Piece of pipe

Bucket

to direct the liquid into a bucket, supported by, for example, a piece of metal tubing; or b) make a raised partition in the form of a wooden grid in the bottom container.

- Before you make the grid make a large hole in the container for the liquid to drain from, or fit a tap to the container.

- To make the raised layer attach two battens across each of the longest sides, using self-tapping screws, about 4 inches from the bottom. Then fix rails supported by these battens with a half-centimetre gap between each, forming a raised grid across the bottom of the container. On top of this put a section of a polypropylene woven mesh, which will stop worms falling through but allow the liquid to drain.

- Set the base container up on a couple of concrete blocks (or similar), open the tap if fitted, and put a bucket ready to catch liquid.

- Put a generous layer of compost/leafmould on top of the mesh or in the bottom of the container and your worms on top of that – you can cover them with a 'moisture mat' (you can buy this matting as capillary matting from garden centres or just use a couple of sheets of wetted newspaper). Put the lid on.

- Let the worms settle in for a couple of days and then start to feed them very small amounts at first.

- When the first container is about three-quarters full, take the lid off and put the second container on top. Level the contents first so that the new container makes good contact. Put a thin layer of finished compost/leafmould in this next container and continue adding your food scraps, etc.

- Repeat the above stage with the third container – the worms will continually work their way upwards.

- When the top container is getting full you can remove the top two containers and empty the base and the middle container out.

- Reprime the base container with some of the material from the middle one and replace the top container, which will now become the middle container.

Half barrel

The simplest containers often seem to work the best (I have a large plastic barrel sawn in half, which makes two great wormeries). You can often find barrels fairly easily, but make sure you get only ones that contained safe materials – barrels that contained fruit juice are excellent and you can often find them advertised in the small ads or even at your local garden centre, as they make great water butts too.

A half barrel with holes drilled in the bottom makes a simple wormery. You can drain the leachate off using a piece of plastic and some metal tubing.

- Saw the barrel in half, either across the middle or lengthwise, to make two containers – but bear in mind that you really want a well-fitting lid.

- Find something to use as a lid. (I have a selection of old dustbin lids I've acquired from skip rummaging, but any cover that will keep the rain out will do.)

- Drill plenty of holes in the bottom for drainage.

- Set the half barrel up on blocks so that it will drain efficiently. If you want you can put a piece of plastic sheeting underneath to divert liquids into a bucket, as in the stacking system.

Old freezer

My freezer is also set up on blocks and has a drainage hole with a bucket underneath. At the bottom of the freezer is a wooden grid, as described in 'Stacking wormery', page 74, so that liquids can drain away more easily.

Wheelie bin

You can use a wheelie bin and fit a tap in it – leave the tap open with a bucket to catch the liquid. I prefer drilling a hole and putting in a short length of pipe to direct the liquid into a bucket, as it's easier to clean out and simpler to fit. You will still need to fit a grid above the tap.

Old degassed chest freezers make great wormeries.

Preparing for your worms' arrival

Siting your wormery

You can site your wormery just about anywhere, but worms don't like to get too hot or too cold, so don't put it in a sun trap or a freezing cold place. My insulated deep freezer is ideal as it keeps the worms warm in winter and cool in summer and, because it is insulated, it can go where I want regardless of sun or shade.

Bedding

No matter which container you use, you must start the worms off with a generous bedding layer, at least 10cm deep. Bedding can be leafmould, finished compost (preferably sieved), shredded-up newspaper and/or well-rotted sawdust or wood-chip, or a mixture of any or all of these. Whatever it is, it must be thoroughly wetted – especially paper and cardboard, as worms will die if they dry out.

Getting your worms

Now you've got somewhere for them to live, all you need is your worms! Don't be tempted to dig worms out of the soil in your garden for your wormery: they will not be the right ones. The soil-burrowing worms, principally *Lumbricus terrestris*, are the large mauve-coloured worms that Charles Darwin devoted a large part of his life to studying, and they do not live in compost heaps, although you some-times find them in leaf-mould piles.

You need compost worms for your wormery: these are naturally occurring litter-, compost- and manure-dwelling worms. There are many different species of these, including red ones and stripy ones. The most common species of worm found in manures and compost heaps is probably *Eisenia fetida* – it has the common names of brandling and tiger worm. If you buy composting worms they are often a different species, *Dendrobaena veneta* (commonly called blue-nose worms), or you may get a mixture of various species. The Latin classification of the natural world is generally used for universal clarification – however, in the case of worms it is very difficult to accurately identify individual species and there is much confusion over names. It seems that different Latin and common names are often given for the same worms – gardeners are used to plants having different Latin and common names, and the same is true of worms.

It doesn't really matter too much what sort of compost worms they are, however: if you can find worms in your compost heap or manure pile then they are the right ones. If you order them from a supplier they will supply the right worms for the job too.

You can start a wormery off with a small amount of worms – in theory just two individuals – but the more the better, and worm suppliers will generally start at about half a kilo. As long as the worms are happy they will soon multiply, but of course you will only be able to put in very small amounts of food until they have really multiplied.

The alternative is to buy in enough worms to really kick-start your wormery into action – at least 500 but preferably 1,000 worms should do the job. Up to a point the more worms you have, the faster it all happens. But the other limiting factor to the speed of composting is the size of the surface area of your bin or container. (That's why commercial worm farm beds look like raised garden beds, i.e. a horizontal system, which take up much more space than the vertical wormeries on sale for domestic use).

So if you have masses of worms and just one container, why not split the colony in half and set up a second bin and progress to having a whole series of bins? That way you will be able to process more material.

Most of the companies that supply wormeries will also sell you worms. They arrive in a container through the post, ready for action. Get them straight into the wormery as soon as they arrive. Do NOT leave them hanging around in a warm place in their bag, or they will die! Suppliers are listed in the Resources section of this book.

Using your wormery

If you are putting fresh material in, you can add only very small amounts at a time as the worms can eat it only when it starts to decompose. So when you are feeding fresh material directly to your worms it is vital that you do not put so much in that it starts to compost and heat up. A wormery is not really composting at all – think of it as farming worms; the product is the worm poo (called worm casts).

If you are using material from your tumbler, which has already been through the hot stage of the composting process (see Chapter 2) and is cooling down, you can put whole loads into your wormery as the worms will be able to process the material straight away.

This is the major difference between worm farming on a larger scale and on a small domestic scale. Worm farmers will take whole loads of fresh material and compost it until the heat has died down, then spread it out on worm beds to be matured and finished by the worms.

Feeding your worms

> *"Worms can eat about half their own weight in food each day."* – The Worm Research Centre

Think of your worm bin as a mini farm; do not treat it as if it is a dustbin.

- After you have introduced the worms into the container, let them settle down for a day or two. They will be quite happy eating their bedding.

- **Don't put too much in a wormery at any time** – a pile of fresh grass cuttings, for example, will smother the worms. They don't want a great pile of stuff dumped on them, as it can compost and generate heat – and they like it cool! If you have large amounts of food waste then you cannot expect a wormery to deal with it without hot composting it first. Overfeeding is a common reason why wormeries fail. Little and often is best, particularly when you first start and the colony is growing – handfuls rather than bucketfuls.

- Wormeries are ideal for *small* amounts of 'difficult' kitchen materials – food scraps, cooked leftovers, meat and fish, cheese rinds, bread, etc. It's best to avoid or bury any fresh meat or fish in the wormery so as not to attract blowflies.

- Worms eat rotting matter, and are particularly useful because they will eat not only all your food waste but also some paper and cardboard. You can line your kitchen caddy with newspaper or cardboard and put envelopes, toilet roll centres, old kitchen paper and so on in your caddy, and get the right mix before it even goes into the wormery.

- You will find other authorities telling you to avoid certain foodstuffs in your wormery, e.g. oily food, dairy, meat, eggs. In fact, however, the worms will eat all this stuff; it's just that these things tend to be hanging around for a long time rotting before the worms can process them, and in this time can be attracting flies and other undesirable creatures. (This is another good reason to 'hot compost' these materials first if at all possible; see Chapter 2, page 28.)

- Separate out your materials so that fresh vegetable trimmings mostly go in your compost heap and the kitchen scraps go in the wormery, then you won't create masses of liquid and generate heat.

Caring for your worms

Think of the worms as your pets, not as a composting system!

- Worms like their home to be cool and moist, but not too cold. They will not be very active at low temperatures, and if it gets too hot they will climb out if they can.

- Tap off the liquid and clean out the tap every time you empty your wormery to prevent your worms drowning. If they get too wet, they may drown or simply leave to try to find a better home.

- You can add some 'structural' material such as woodchip (even though some wormery instructions tell you not to), because it helps to keep the contents aerobic (with-air). I add woodchip to my food waste tumbling systems, as my wormeries are all used to mature the food waste and I then don't get the sometimes rather anaerobic smell you can get from a wormery when you get down to the dense 'chocolate fudge cake' casts at the bottom of a bin.

- You will often find little white worms, sometimes in great quantities, in your wormery – these are *Enchytraeid* worms – also known as white worms or pot worms; while they are beneficial they do indicate that your wormery is getting too acidic. If this happens, add some rock dust or garden lime – preferably limestone flour, which you can buy as a mineral supplement for horses (usually available from any place selling horsey equipment and feed). Do *not* add builders' lime!

- Be patient – your wormery will probably take at least a year to get up to full speed as the worms breed. You can expect 15,000-20,000 worms in your wormery by then!

The finished product

Harvesting your worm compost

Wormeries take a long time to fill up, and underneath the main mass of worms will be their manure, called 'worm casts'. When the container is getting pretty full it's time to harvest – choose a nice warm, preferably sunny, day.

- Remove the freshest material plus the layer immediately underneath – this should contain a rich seam of worms.

- Put all this to one side. It will go back into your wormery when you have harvested the worm casts.

- Dig out or tip out the rest – all the rich dark material at the bottom, which is pretty well all worm casts by now.

- If you want to save every last worm to put back in your wormery, spread the bottom material out in a layer on a large sheet of plastic or a tarpaulin, etc. and then make a series of little conical piles all over the sheet. (If you don't want to do this don't worry, as there shouldn't be too many worms in the lower levels.)

Have a tea break!

- Now pick off all the tops of the piles and put them in a bucket. At the base of each pile you should find the worms getting as far away from the light as possible.

- If you examine your worm compost closely you should also find the worm cocoons, which contain the baby worms and are similar in size and shape to grape pips – but it's a big job picking these out. I don't bother but I know people who do!

- You can put all the worms and cocoons back into your wormery or start off a fresh colony in a new container.

If you have a stacking system, you merely remove and empty the bottom container, and place it back on the top of the wormery. The whole cycle then starts again.

Using worm casts

Worm casts (the name given to the finished worm compost) are the crème de la crème of composts, and are best used by the handful rather than the wheelbarrow load. Think of worm casts as fertiliser, not compost: a little goes a long way. Give all your pot plants, window boxes and hanging baskets a top dressing. Water them thoroughly first, and then top-dress with a handful or so of worm casts. You can do the same with garden plants – as a no-dig gardener I just top-dress with worm casts (see Chapter 6), but you could incorporate the worm casts into the top layer of soil.

I've recently been using my worm casts to make an extract (see *Worm casts* and *Compost extracts* in the A–Z Guide).

> ### *Worms grind and crush up bacteria*
>
> Worms are incredible in that they clean up any nasty pathogenic bacteria that could be in your wormery or compost. Since they naturally invade compost heaps during the maturation phase of composting, they are doing several great jobs simultaneously. They have gizzards that crush microscopic organisms to extract the nutrients. In fact Elaine Ingham (see Soil Food Web in the Resources section) says that in one experiment a single worm was placed on a Petri dish contaminated with e-coli for 20 minutes. After the worm was removed no e-coli was found on the dish.

Using the liquid fertiliser

The liquid that you drain off from your wormery makes a wonderful liquid feed for all your plants, especially fruit. You can leave the tap of your wormery open all the time and put a small bucket underneath it, which prevents the container gradually filling up with liquid and drowning your worms.

- Dilute with *at least* ten parts water before using as a foliar feed or around the roots of your plants. Think of the water as a carrier for your microbe-rich liquid rather than as a dilution.

- The water with the worm liquid in should be barely coloured.

- Adding a drop or two of soft soap or eco washing liquid will break the water tension and coat your plants with a heady mix of beneficial nutrients and microorganisms.

- As with all foliar feeding, make sure that you do not do this in full sun – early morning or late evening is best. (Also see *Compost tea* and *Compost extract* in the A–Z Guide.)

CHAPTER 6

USING YOUR COMPOST

'Compost' is a word with two meanings:

- On the one hand it is the material that results from the composting process and is used to enrich and improve your soil.

- On the other hand it means a 'composition' of different materials mixed together to make what is more commonly referred to as a 'growing medium'. This growing medium may actually be composed of completely artificial ingredients, and I often refer to it as 'peat in a bag with chemicals'. You can make your own growing media by combining your compost with other naturally occurring materials (see page 89).

Using compost in a no-dig garden

The Henry Doubleday site I worked on as a student in the 1980s had demonstration gardens of different systems. I was put in charge of the John Jeavons system, which involved double digging the beds. I used to look across enviously during this back-breaking work to my colleague Pat gently hoeing around his no-dig beds, and swore that I would be a no-dig gardener in future.

I've been striving to be a no-dig gardener, or at least a minimal-dig gardener, for many years now. You need a lot of material to set up a no-dig system, as you need 3 or 4 inches of compost on each bed, which translates pretty quickly into a hefty tonnage. It was this desire to have lots of compost that opened my eyes to realising that all kinds of commonly wasted materials could be used to make more compost.

You can buy compost in quantity, from some local authorities and commercial composting businesses, but you have to pay both for the compost and the haulage – and ideally you need good access to move the compost as close as possible to where you need it. I became a community composter (see Resources section) in part so that I could get my hands on more compost without having to pay for it! I also strive to be a no-dig gardener because digging is counterproductive in many ways.

The advantages of a no-dig garden

• You maintain earthworm aeration tunnels, do not slice the worms in half, and do not disturb the ecology of the soil.

• You are helping to sequester carbon in the soil. By digging you increase the amount of oxygen in the soil, which oxidises more of the carbon, releasing it as carbon dioxide. Never before has it been so vital for us to 'bank' as much carbon in the form of humus in our soils. (Also see *Biochar* in the A–Z Guide.)

• You help to maintain the fertility and water-holding capacity of your soil.

• You do not expose weed seeds to the light, where they are triggered into germinating. Some of these seeds can remain for decades under your soil – think of the poppy fields of Flanders, where seeds were brought into the light from the shelling.

• Perennial weed roots are not cut up and potentially multiplied.

• The layer directly under the depth of your spade is not 'panned', causing a hard layer that is impenetrable by plant roots. This is more common on soils that have been ploughed using heavy machinery or rotovated.

• You can use uncomposted organic materials without fear of 'nitrogen robbery', as these materials will only gradually be incorporated into the soil – see box.

Nitrogen robbery

If you dig materials into the soil that are high in carbon, such as sawdust or wood chippings, the nitrogen in the soil, rather than being available to feed plants, instead becomes involved in de-composing the carbon. *This process ideally needs to take place in the compost heap, not the soil.* Eventually the carbon will break down with the help of the nitrogen and the soil will be rich in humus, but during the decomposition process plants with roots in the top layer of soil will be starved of vital nutrients. Sawdust, which has a massive surface area, will cause much more nitrogen robbery than will a piece of wood in the soil.

However, you can add high-carbon materials (bark chips, cardboard, woodchip, straw and so on) to the soil surface, even directly around shallow-rooted plants. This is because only a very small surface area of the high-carbon materials is in contact with the soil, and only a small proportion of nitrogen is involved in converting it into humus.

In order to become a no-dig gardener you do need plenty of organic materials. Luckily, however, there is no shortage of compostable material and many people are keen to dump it. Just look around and see how much organic material there is available, which could be turned into compost or used as a mulch.

Alternatively, why not grow plants just to compost? Sunflowers and Jerusalem artichokes are good, so are nettles and bracken; they will add bulk to your compost heap and be a good mix of fibre (dryer carbon-rich matter and green sappy nitrogen-rich matter, which will compost really well). Sow them close together and cut down when only about three feet high.

Creating a no-dig garden with compost

I've set up many no-dig systems now and am always amazed at how simple it is. Here is just one way of doing it.

- If setting up on grassy or weedy ground, scythe or mow and rake the debris to one side. If the ground is clear then skip this step!

- Lay well-rotted manure in long narrow strips about a foot wide and 4-6 inches deep.

- Make a series of these strips about 4-5 feet apart.

My children (Hazel and Kesella) helping create a no-dig garden from scratch using barrier mulching -- raking the grass and laying it on newspaper.

- Plant potatoes along each strip.

- Cover with straw and old hay – this should spill over the foot-wide strip so you end up with beds about three feet wide.

- Sprinkle the fresh grass cuttings back on top if you have them, or try to find grass cuttings to sprinkle on the top.

- Maintenance: mow between the rows and put all the fresh cuttings back on top of the hay as the potatoes emerge to prevent the light from reaching the potatoes.

When I did this it worked extremely well; I had a few green potatoes at the end of the season but they were incredibly easy to harvest and I had established nice long beds ready to plant up with the next crop.

You can also create raised beds with this system. You can make your own with all kinds of scrap (or new wood) – old scaffold boards from scaffolding firms are a good source, or buy actual raised-bed sides in modular form from gardening catalogues or sites, e.g. Garden Organic, Recycle Works or Harrod Horticultural. This makes a neat contained system which you can intensively cultivate as soon as you have a good concentration of compost.

If you are creating a no-dig garden it pays to have a really large amount of compost (one system I set up took 30 tonnes!) – but you can do it with quite small amounts

No-dig beds marked out for the barrier mulch of newspaper and grass – compost will be put on top.

by using a technique called 'barrier mulching'. I helped a friend with her allotment that was becoming too overwhelming for her by this method, as follows.

- We cut the worst of the weeds down.

- We spread really large sheets of cardboard directly on to these undug weedy areas – this is the 'barrier layer'.

- We made little mounds of compost about 18 inches to 2 feet across.

- On each mound we planted a courgette or squash plant.

- On another part we put potatoes in tyres and tomatoes in home-made growbags.

- Watering was essential for maintenance, but it is incredible how much water finished compost will hold.

My friend's no-dig allotment. Top left: cardboard barrier with a mound of compost and two squash plants – I usually plant two or three as an insurance against slugs. Top right: later one squash plant was removed. Bottom left: the mounds are close enough together to almost join up and cover the cardboard – later the compost was spread out and oriental salads sown for the winter. Bottom right: tyres and a section of drainage pipe contain the compost more effectively than a loose mound.

- Once the plants were established they covered the whole area and most weeds were held back.

- Some weeds, like docks, punched their way through the barrier but could be pulled out really easily.

Doing it this way, with cardboard, you make your compost go further and really concentrate it where you need it. The cardboard forms a barrier and kills off most of the grasses and perennial weeds and really helps clear the ground. As it rots you can either weed out the really tough weeds that have survived, or top up the cardboard for a second 'hit'.

Once you've set up a no-dig system you can just continue to add your compost as a mulch to the surface around your plants as they are growing. The earthworms soon incorporate it all in the soil.

Using compost in a conventionally dug garden

Of course compost can be used in any garden, and you can incorporate it into the soil using a rotovator, hand cultivator, fork or spade. All soils benefit from liberal applications of compost or well-rotted manure, whether in a dig or no-dig system. One or two wheelbarrow loads per 5 square metres is the recommendation from Garden Organic (see Resources section).

Mulching

Even gardeners who dig cannot dig everywhere; for instance, around perennial plants it is nearly always best to apply mulches. You can use a barrier mulch, as described above, around perennials that have become invaded by weeds, and compost is just one material you can use in this situation. You can also use wood or bark chips, for instance. However, where you need to feed the plants as well, compost is best. It's always advisable to add mulches after heavy rainfall or a really good soaking.

Top dressing

Top dressing with compost around growing plants is best done after rain or a good soaking and will benefit all crops; if you have set up a no-dig garden you need to maintain it with regular top dressings of compost, ideally an inch at a time.

Woody mulch on one of my paths with a painted lady butterfly.

Using compost on plants in containers

You can also use your compost on any plants in containers of any sort, including indoor houseplants, patio tubs and window boxes. If the plant is an established perennial then it will benefit from a generous top dressing. Always thoroughly soak the plant in the container if possible before adding the top dressing. I try to top-dress all my plants in containers as soon as the growing season is under way, but any time during the season is fine.

Alternatively, if you are moving your plants up a pot size you can often carefully remove some of the old compost and replace with fresh potting compost; water the plant thoroughly and add a layer to the top.

Using worm compost (worm casts)

Worm compost (known as worm casts) is especially rich, so think quality not quantity – a little goes a long way. I find it particularly useful to use worm casts as top dressing (as described on page 87) for containerised plants, especially those needing a bit of a feeding. You can use your worm compost anywhere you have plants and to really make it go further you can mix it with water and apply as a drench or foliar feed – see *Compost tea* in the A–Z Guide.

Potting compost

This relates to the second definition of compost at the beginning of this chapter – i.e. a growing medium composed of different materials.

A potting mix, like a good soil, needs to simultaneously hold moisture and be free draining – which sounds like a paradox. You cannot expect your home-made compost, the final product of your composting process, to have all these qualities, and you will need to add other materials to make a good mix. Many plants need a really free-draining medium, and compost alone can cause waterlogging. Young plants, especially seedlings, do not want a rich mixture, and so the compost needs to be 'diluted' with leafmould or soil. Some plants need a more alkaline medium, and so limestone can be added to the mix.

Finished compost – especially the compost from wormeries – is often quite dense, so you need to add something structural to create air and water channels. I usually use horticultural sands and grits, depending on the size of plant and container. The proportions vary according to the type of plant. Plants that cannot tolerate any waterlogging, for example succulents and cacti, will need a very open mix with plenty of grit and sand. You can also use other materials to open up the mix, such as pearlite and vermiculite.

Try sieving some of your own mature compost (see overleaf) – once the stones, sticks and clumps have gone it should look something like this.

Ingredients that make up a good compost or 'growing medium'

- Sharp sand (always use sharp sand, not builders' sand)
- Grit
- Vermiculite
- Pearlite
- Soil*
- Leafmould
- Minerals, e.g. dolomite and other rock dusts and/or seaweed meal
- Fertilisers, e.g. blood, fish and bone

* Good loam is best. This is a rich, healthy soil with a good mix of sand, silt, clay and organic matter. Being not at all organised I have used the soil in the fields from molehills – which is beautifully prepared by the moles! – but the weed seeds are not killed off. I have also used the soil from my perennial weed and loam stacks (see A–Z Guide). Soil can have a lot of seeds which will germinate and so can cause a problem, especially in seed compost, and so it's good to kill off these seeds by heating up the soil and pasteurising it. Pasteurised soil is soil that has been heated to 60-70°C for a minimum of half an hour to kill weed seed and plant pathogens – you can do this in a domestic oven or a microwave, but you may not be too popular if you do! If you are really clever you can do it by using a hot compost heap, which can reach these temperatures. You will need the temperature to reach mid-60s Celsius right to the centre.

Sieving your compost

You really must sieve your compost for making up potting mixes – but this is quite fun to do, just to see how wonderful your own home-made compost actually is! So many times people have told me that their compost is useless, nothing like the commercially made stuff. This is nonsense! Most of the time all you need to do to make your compost look like the stuff you buy in bags is to sieve it.

However, sieving can be very laborious with a small sieve. If you can find a friend to help you, get hold of a length of chicken wire and hold it so that it forms a U a foot or so from the ground. While one of you holds the chicken wire the other one puts a forkful of compost at a time on to it. Then you rock the wire up and down, rolling the compost through. The big bits you just flick to one side. You can also do this straight into a wheelbarrow, which then becomes a mixing vessel.

Left: a pile of sieved compost from the Proper Job community site in Chagford, piled in the polytunnel to dry out a bit. Top right: this compost is then hand-sieved and mixed with sharp sand and leafmould to make a seed-sowing mix. Bottom right: however, this is not ideal for seeds as it tends to have weed seeds in it, so you have to be good at cotyledon seedling identification!

Some examples of home-made potting mixes

Potting mix 1

This mix is good for a range of plants that like a humus-rich media and are not too fussy about drainage, e.g. most vegetable plants, tomatoes, squashes, brassicas, legumes, etc., and it gives an ideal environment for them until they are ready to be planted out.

- 1 part soil* (see note in box opposite). I generally use soil without pasteurising it and pick out any weeds which come up, which is OK for potting composts – but not seed composts!)

- 2 parts sieved compost.

- 1 part vermiculite.

Potting mix 2

This is more of a light, general-purpose mix, which I use for a wide variety of flowers, herbs and houseplants – for example, pinks, dianthus, pansies, thyme, etc.

- 1 part soil* (see note in box opposite).

- 1 part sieved compost.

- 1 part leafmould.

Potting mix 3
This is more suitable for houseplants, window boxes and containers.

*   2 parts soil* (see note in box on page 90).

*   1 part sieved compost.

*   1 part sharp sand.

I have even used my own sieved compost neat for potting up some plants, usually just for a short period, but I wouldn't really recommend it as it can be too dense on its own and really needs some grit, vermiculite or pearlite to open it up.

Compost for cuttings

If you want a mix for cuttings you need a really open, free-draining compost that nevertheless still holds on to moisture, and you don't want it to be too nutrient-rich, which can lead to soft, sappy growth. Leafmould is very low in nutrients and when mixed half-and-half with sharp sand it is very good – but if you don't have leafmould you *can* use your own compost mixed with the same proportion of sharp sand.

For slower-rooting cuttings try:

*   1 part pasteurised soil (pulling out weeds that have germinated around cuttings that are trying to root can ruin your cuttings)

*   2 parts leafmould.

*   1 part sharp sand.

Seed compost

Making seed compost from your own compost is tricky because of the likelihood that you will almost certainly not have killed all the weed seeds.
    However, you can make a seed compost by layering grass mowings with cardboard:

*   Alternate very thin layers (an inch or so) of freshly cut grass with a layer of corrugated cardboard. At this ratio there is just enough air and absorption in the cardboard to mop up the juices from the grass and aerate the grass; you can do this in any garden composter

- When it starts to slump down, dig it out, mix it up and re-stack it. This will result in a peat-like substitute, like leafmould – I call it cardboard mould.

- Use two parts leafmould or 'cardboard mould' with one part sharp sand to make up your seed compost.

Water the seedlings with seaweed extract to provide essential minerals – they should be moved out (pricked out) of the seed compost into a potting mix when they have their first true leaves.

Artichoke seedlings. When you can see roots poking out of the bottom of the modules the seedlings can be transferred into individual pots.

CHAPTER 7

COMMUNITY COMPOSTING

In 1992 I was inspired to get some people together to start a community composting scheme, after seeing the amount of material people were piling into the bulky household skips the council brought to our community every month. Just about everything from the garden was being piled into these skips, from bags of grass cuttings to leaves, weeds, prunings, branches, soil and even lovely plants. Over the years I've rescued many wonderful plants that people have just thrown away – my peony collection comes from throw-outs. My other motivation for the scheme was to offer a service to my fellow allotment-holders so that they didn't have so many choking bonfires all the time.

I believe that every community should have a community composting scheme. It's just crazy to burn or dispose of all these potentially compostable materials, and even crazier to load it on to lorries and drive it miles away, even if it is going to be composted at some municipal compost site – though this is admittedly better than the old system of burying it in the ground.

In the early 1990s a few other like-minded souls were also running community schemes as wide-ranging as Scotland, Wales, Kent, Skegness and the Forest of Dean. The Community Composting Network (CCN) was formed in 1995 and now there are schemes not only all over the UK but also in Europe, and there is even a scheme in Sierra Leone.

Types of community project

Community composting projects come in all shapes and sizes. The following are some examples. (For information on all these projects and more see the Community Composting Network website in the Resources section.)

- Inner-city schemes collecting food waste on estates (e.g. the East London Community Recycling Project in Hackney and Aardvark in Southwark, South London).

Top left: food-waste bins with locking handles left out for collection in London. Top right: stockpiling woody clippings prior to shredding at Chudleigh Rotters community composting site. Bottom left: large piles covered up and gently composting at Lympstone community composting site. Bottom right: special needs volunteers emptying the sacks from the collection round vehicle on to the current compost pile.

- Schemes working with all manner of marginalised people in society. This includes the long-term unemployed (e.g. Seagull in Skegness), recovering addicts (e.g. the Coach House project in Glasgow), and people with learning disabilities (e.g. Colington Compost in Edinburgh) or mental health problems. These schemes offer meaningful and therapeutic employment as well as offering a great service to their local community.

- Some schemes diversify into all manner of areas, from growing food (e.g. the [Forest of] Dean Community Compost), collecting on behalf of their local authority (e.g. WyeCycle in Kent) or running reuse and recycling sites as well (e.g. Proper Job, Chagford, Devon).

- Some projects are very small – this is true of most of the projects in Devon and many other rural projects all over the UK.

How do you get started?

Most of the projects I've been involved with have usually started from an initial enquiry from either an individual or someone representing a group, such as their allotment group or parish council. People generally come to me with the idea that a community composting project just means having a communal pile somewhere that everyone can easily bring stuff to. The reality is a little more complex!

You will need:

1. **Support:** A successful scheme needs support from the community and commitment from a hard-core group of enthusiasts. Some sort of consultation with the community is advisable, as not everybody likes the idea of a composting project on their doorstep, so you do need to do your homework first, and get prepared to answer awkward questions.

2. **Information:** Look at the Community Composting Network's website and, if you are in Devon, take a look at the Devon Community Composting Network's (DCCN) website too (see Resources section).

3. **Funding:** In order to get any funding the group generally has to adopt a constitution, or become a subgroup of an existing group (such as the parish council or allotment society).

4. **A site:** You will need to find a suitable site, which will be acceptable to the Environment Agency and the planners. Again, talk to CCN first.

5. **Research:** Talk to other community composters before you get too far on with your plans and, if possible, visit an existing project. The CCN has demon-

stration sites all over the country. You could just make contact with your nearest and visit them, but bear in mind that you need to find the right model for your situation and there is a huge diversity of different types of project, so maybe your nearest one might not be exactly the model that you would like to emulate.

So many new groups are springing up around the country, including climate change groups and Transition town groups, and many of them could form a composting group as part of their activities. So if there's no scheme near you, why not start one?

Members of Chudleigh Rotters community composting team on their allotments, showing off their New Zealand bins and the Devon Rotary sieve (designed and built by Sam Seward) between the banks of bays.

PART TWO

CHAPTER 8

A–Z GUIDE

Acidity (*see also Alkalinity, pH*)
Some materials, e.g. citrus fruit, are very acid, and if you are composting these in large quantities then adding ground limestone is the easiest way to counter the effect. Generally, though, just mixing with plenty of other material is better, as the raising of pH by adding lime to the composting process tends to result in nitrogen being released as ammonia gas (see *Alkalinity*). The composting process generally starts off fairly acid, with a low pH, and finished compost is slightly alkaline.

Activated charcoal (*see also Charcoal, Biochar, Kitchen caddies*)
Charcoal that has been processed with oxygen to open up the structure can result in a surface area of 300-2,000 square metres *per gram*! This is why it is used in odour-control filters for compost caddies and some composting systems.

Activators
An activator is something added to a compost heap to speed up the composting process. However, compost made correctly doesn't generally need an activator. Commercially available activators are generally either chemical nitrogen, which can have a detrimental effect on the microorganisms in the heap, or a bacterial culture.

If you want to introduce more bacteria, the best and easiest way is to add some of your old mature or maturing compost, if you have some, or add the odd light sprinkling of soil, which will introduce countless millions of bacteria.

However, if you do want to use an activator there are various options.

- *Urine*. This is probably the cheapest and best (preferably dilute 1:4 with water). It adds nitrogen and water to woody, dry, carbon-rich material.

- *Grass cuttings*. In thin layers these are excellent – very similar to urine, i.e. high in nitrogen and water.

- *Manures*. Layer or mix into the heap. Remember that manures are pretty strong, with a high level of nitrogen (this is especially true of chicken manure), so always try to break them up, and add in thin layers.

- *Nettles*. These compost extremely well, and are a valuable addition to any compost heap, but don't add the roots as you may get nettles growing instead of composting.

- Any other dynamic accumulators (see *Dynamic accumulators*), such as comfrey, chamomile, valerian, the tops of deep-rooting weeds such as dandelions, etc., will to add both nitrogen and valuable minerals.

- *Coffee grounds*. Coffee grounds and beans are great in compost, as coffee has a microporous structure like charcoal and contains a wide range of useful microorganisms – if you can get grounds in quantity, so much the better.

- *Seaweed*. Use either freshly harvested (don't pick up old seaweed, which will have accumulated high concentrations of salt; either harvest at low tide or go out after a storm, when plenty will be washed up), as liquid concentrate, or as a dried meal. Seaweed is a rich source of trace elements, which are vital for soils and humans, and is particularly rich in potassium and nitrogen.

- *Biodynamic preparations*. Biodynamic gardeners and farmers, who follow the teachings of Rudolph Steiner, put special herbal preparations into their heap; these plants are also dynamic accumulators. They can be bought from the Biodynamic Agricultural Association (see Resources section, page 183).

- *QR (Quick Return)*. The six plants that the biodynamic growers use – dandelion, yarrow, nettle, oak bark, valerian and chamomile – form the basis of the QR ('Quick Return') preparation that Maye Bruce, a founder member of the Soil Association, developed in the 1930s. She wrote several books about her experiments (see Resources, page 179). She realised that for most people making the proper biodynamic preparations would just not be feasible, and so made a version of her own that you can still buy today from The Organic Gardening Catalogue (see www.organiccatalogue.com). You just put a teaspoonful of the powdered herbs in some warm water with some honey and let it brew for a while. Then you add it to the compost pile. Be careful if you add these herbs as live plants, since some are quite pernicious weeds, and small bits of root, not properly composted, could take hold and thrive in your compost.

- You can also buy various proprietary activators for individual materials, e.g. for grass cuttings, leafmould, etc. I've never found the need to try any of these products so I cannot vouch for them personally. Grass cuttings are dead easy to compost and leaves just take time.

Additives (*see also Acidity, Rock dust, Weeds*)
Various materials can be added to composting and wormery systems to supply missing nutrients or to balance the acidity.

- *Limestone.* Compost heaps and wormeries that are too wet and airless become smelly and acidic. By adding more dry material and some limestone you will help correct the balance. Limestone flour is the most finely ground and effective, and can be bought in small bags as a mineral supplement for animals – look for suppliers of horse feed. Limestone counteracts acidity, but it must never be sprinkled directly on to manures, as you will get a reaction releasing ammonia and nitrogen as a gas. **Do not use builders' lime, also known as quicklime or hydrated lime.**

- *Rock dust,* e.g. dolomite, which contains calcium and magnesium, is useful to correct over-acidity in wormeries and other kitchen waste systems.

- *Wood ash and soot* are rich alkali sources, but don't add to a heap in great dollops or it will turn to a horrible sludge; instead scatter it and mix in well.

- *Crushed up bones and eggshells* – see *Bones* and *Shells*.

Adsorption (*see also Cation exchange capacity, Humus, Soil types*)
Adsorption in the soil is the attraction of positively charged compounds or ions (very small particles, in this case cations), to negatively charged clay or humus particles, which results in the cations being held on the surface of the clay or humus particles. (This is in contrast to *ab*sortion, which is where liquids permeate into a material.)

Aerobic (*see also Air*)
This means 'with air', one of the four essentials for making good compost.

Air (*see also 'Browns'*)
For composting to work there *must* be sufficient air for the organisms that are living in the compost heap to thrive. The air is primarily contained in the 'brown' materials you add to the heap and the air spaces they create as they decompose; especially useful are woodchippings or shreddings, as they provide little air pockets as the heap sinks down. (See also the 'four-word mantra', Chapter 2, page 21).

Alkalinity
Unless you are adding a lot of highly acidic materials to your compost then it is not generally a good idea to add highly alkaline materials, such as lime or ash, and certainly not in any quantity. Alkaline materials will react with high-nitrogen materials such as fresh manures, which results in nitrogen being released into the atmosphere as ammonia.

Aminopyralid (*see also Clopyralid, Manure*)
This is a chemical weedkiller that is extremely resistant to being broken down in the composting process.

Anaerobic
This means 'absence of air' and is what happens to compost when, for instance, you make a pile of grass cuttings. The mass heats up and starts to collapse and pack all the air spaces together, until only the smelly 'anaerobic' bacteria can survive – to give composting a bad name. There are, however, good anaerobic microorganisms and microorganisms that are involved in fermentation that may be present with or without oxygen (see *Bokashi*).

Anions (*see also Cation exchange capacity, Humus*)
Pronounced 'an-iron', these are negatively charged ions (very small particles). They are not held in the soil by humus or clay particles, but are consumed and held in the soil by the microbial flora and fauna, and thus made available to plants. Examples of anions include nitrate and phosphate, which are forms of two of the major nutrients needed by plants, nitrogen and phosphorus. Anions tend to leach (see *Compost leachate*) as they are not held by adsorption.

Ants
A few ants in the compost heap are not doing any harm; in fact they are probably helping it – I've had wonderfully fine-sifted compost all done by ants. If you want to harvest the compost, give it a good watering the day before and the ants will, hopefully, move out. However, if you live near woodland and wood ants invade your heap, they will probably steal your entire heap, and if you put compost out as a mulch around your plants, they will steal all that too. I know – it happened to me; in the end I moved house!

Michael Braungart (co-author of *Cradle to Cradle*) says that the combined biomass of ants on the planet is equivalent to the human population. Guess which of the two species has a net benefit to the planet's ecosystems!

Ash *see Activators, Coal ash, Wood ash, Alkalinity*

Autumn leaves (*see also Leaves and leafmould*)
Leaves are so easy to compost and so good for the garden that you really shouldn't burn them – collect them to make leafmould (see page 38).

Barrier mulch *see Mulches and barrier mulches*

Bindweed *see Pernicious weeds*

Bioaerosols (*see also Turning*)
Airborne microscopic organic particles, such as pollen and fungal spores, are

called bioaerosols, and dry or musty compost heaps can release huge quantities of them when turned and can be dangerous causing allergic reactions in very rare cases. Of most concern is *Aspergillus fumigatus* – these spores can lodge and pro-liferate in the lung, leading to the condition known as 'farmer's lung'. So, if you must turn the heap, soak it well before turning, and/or use a proper mask. It is better to just soak the heap well and leave it alone until it has composted down more and the potential danger has passed.

Biochar (*see also Cation exchange capacity, Humus*)
Biochar is the English name for *Terra preta* ('dark earth' in Portugese), a kind of 'slash and char' technique. Early explorers in the Amazon noticed very fertile, deep black soils that had been cultivated over hundreds of years and that these soils contained charcoal. The current method used to clear forest – slash and burn – is a largely uncontrolled burn, which results in carbon being released into the atmos-phere, and a highly soluble ash containing predominately potassium and other nutrients remaining. Crops initially grow very well but after a very short space of time the soil is exhausted and only bare mineral rock remains.

In 'slash and char', on the other hand, the fire is starved of oxygen so charcoal is produced instead, and this charcoal is a very stable form of carbon which has high cation exchange capacity (CEC – see 'Why make compost?', page 16). Charcoal also has a honeycomb structure, a massive surface area, which holds on to water, nutri-ents and soil microorganisms, much as humus does.

Avoid buying charcoal made from tropical rainforests, however – but why not try some locally produced charcoal mixed into your compost? You really want only the smallest particles, so you will have to crush it up before adding it. See http://terrapreta.bioenergylists.org or look on YouTube for more on biochar. The Centre for Alternative Technology has also been running some experiments on biochar and its effect on soils.

(NB Char is the name given to charcoal that is not being used as a fuel. James Lovelock in his book *The vanishing face of Gaia – a final warning*, thinks that the best hope for us to combat climate change is to make enormous amounts of bio-char and to bury it, as this method sequesters carbon most effectively. How practical and effective this would be is open to debate, but nevertheless we could all try it in our gardens and see how effective charcoal in the soil is on the health and welfare of our plants.)

Biodynamic compost (*see also Activators – Quick Return*)
Biodynamic farmers and growers, who follow the teachings of Rudolph Steiner, make six preparations involving plants to be used in the compost heap: dandelion, yarrow, nettle, oak bark, valerian and chamomile. All of these preparations are added to the compost in very small quantities. Biodynamic growers also fill cows' horns with manure, which they bury in the ground on the autumn equinox and dig up on the spring equinox. The contents are then stirred into a bucket of water, creating a deep vortex, and then the stirring is reversed. Then this liquid is sprayed

on to the land. It may sound weird, but if you visit a biodynamic farm or garden I guarantee you will see the most amazing crops being grown.

Bioremediation (*see also Contaminants*)
Contaminated soils, from oil spills, industrial processes and so on can be cleaned of pollutants by specialist companies who use microorganisms, fungi, plants and enzymes. Mixing contaminated soils with large quantities of materials and composting the whole is one system. Paul Stamets (see Websites in Resources section) uses the term 'mycoremediation', as his system uses just fungi to clean up contaminated soil. This is not a something to try with your home composting system.

Bokashi
This is an anaerobic or fermentation system of composting. EM Bokashi (the EM stands for effective microorganisms, and is a mixture of different types of bacteria, actinomycetes and fungi) was developed by Teruo Higa in Japan. See Chapter 4, page 56, for more on Bokashi.)

Bonemeal
Bonemeal is a natural source of phosphorus for the gardener. Some people say that the origin of the word bonfire is a 'fire for bones' – they certainly are a lot easier to grind up when thoroughly dried out or heated up. If you don't grind them up, they take a very long time to break down!

To make bonemeal:

- boil up all bones for stock

- dry out the bones: if you have a cooker that is always on, such as an Aga or Rayburn, put them in the bottom oven or put in any low oven – utilise the heat after cooking, for instance

- remove them from the oven and grind up with a large pestle and mortar – they break up very readily when completely dried out – then use as an additive: sprinkle into your compost or wormery.

Bones
You can put bones into any of the systems dealing with food waste and you will end up with very clean bones, but the large ones will persist in your garden for a very, very long time. That's why it's really best to remove them and follow the instructions for bonemeal, above.

Bracken (*see also Carbon-to-nitrogen ratio*)
Bracken is great stuff to compost and you can make heaps of it when fully unfurled just on its own as it has the right water-to-dry-matter : carbon-to-nitrogen ratio.

Some sources claim that bracken spores may be carcinogenic, but this is based on research on mice, and no link has been established between bracken spores and harm to human health.

Bread
You can put bread – and cake – in any of the cooked-waste composting systems described in this book (see Chapter 4), but you can also try to reduce how much you waste. For example, turn stale bread into breadcrumbs, which can then be mixed with leftover fat to fill coconut halves and put outside to feed the birds. Alternatively, use the bread or breadcrumbs in cooking – croutons, bread sauce, stuffing, etc.

'Browns' (see also Carbon)
This is a generic term for a wide range of carbon-rich materials, which tend to be dry and hard but not necessarily brown! Includes paper, cardboard, dry plant stems, wood and bark chips.

Butter see Dairy food

Caddies see Kitchen caddies

Cake see Bread

Cans
Cans cannot be composted. If you do not have a kerbside collection, recycle them at your local recycling centre.

Carbon (see also 'Browns', Carbon-to-nitrogen ratio, 'Greens', Humus)
Carbon is the main building block of life. In composting terms its most useful common forms are:

- *cellulose*, such as paper, cardboard and the fibrous parts of plants

- *lignins*, which are the denser heartwoods of trees and shrubs.

Materials high in carbon, the 'browns', do not compost readily without being mixed with materials high in nitrogen – the 'greens'. This means that you can stock-pile them safely to be used when needed, unlike the 'green' materials, which really need to be dealt with straight away.

Carbon ('browns') performs three major functions in the compost heap.

- Most importantly, it provides structure to the heap – wood or bark chips are ideal for this.

- Secondly, carbon provides food for the microorganisms as a balance to the nitrogen – this is the carbon-to-nitrogen ratio that composters talk about. Shredded garden clippings, sawdust and shavings are best for this function.

- Thirdly, carbon can absorb liquids released from the breakdown process. Paper and cardboard are ideal for this.

A proportion of carbon most resistant to be being broken down becomes humus in the soil.

Carbon piles (*see also Compost leachate, Humanure composting, Leaves and leafmould, Windrows, Woody materials*)
Because carbon-rich materials can be stored until needed it is useful to create special piles of them – autumn leaves are an example of a high-carbon pile that will happily sit in a simple enclosure for a year, or two or three, quietly being broken down by fungi and made into a wonderfully useful substance – leafmould.

You can also make long-term piles of sawdust, wood or bark chips, twigs/brash, cardboard, etc. Any compost leachate you have, or urine, can be added to these piles and will hasten their decomposition – see pictures on page 50. I get large sacks of shavings and sawdust from a furniture-maker friend (he uses only wood, not any man-made composites such as plywood or MDF, which contain toxic glues and resins), and I collect these shavings until I've filled a bin made from four pallets tied together. They gradually darken and after six months or a year I use them in my humanure system (see page 120), but they are also good with food-waste systems and high-nitrogen systems generally.

Fresh sawdust, shavings and woodchip have the highest carbon-to-nitrogen ratio and are also not very absorbent. However, they become darker and more absorbent when they have been weathered outside for a year in the rain, and maybe had urine and leachate added too, as by then the fibres have opened up somewhat. I prefer to use them at this stage rather than using the fresh sawdust or chip, as long as it is not too wet; it needs to have dried off so that it can be absorbent. In this state it's great to use with food waste and humanure. I'm told that softwoods compost more readily, but as I pre-treat all my sawdust and shavings as described I can't say I've really noticed a difference.

Carbon-to-nitrogen ratio (C:N)
To make the best compost, you need to have the right carbon-to-nitrogen ratio in your heap: the optimum ratio is 25-30:1. The easiest way to understand the correct balance between 'browns' and 'greens', and therefore to get the right ratio, is to look at what the C:N ratios are in some common materials.

- Vegetable waste and grass cuttings are about 12:1, i.e. there are twelve parts carbon to each part of nitrogen – so they are over twice as nitrogen-rich as the optimum ratio.

- At the other end of the scale, fresh sawdust is around 500:1.

- The pods from peas and beans and bracken are 30:1, about perfect to compost on their own – plenty of fibre, and yet still green.

- In practice, just think of one bucket of kitchen waste or grass cuttings to a bucket of shreddings or woodchip.

Cardboard

Large sheets of cardboard (natural-coloured and/or pigmented) are really useful if you have a garden and a large compost heap. Take off all the packing tape and don't use any with plastic coatings, etc.

- Any type of card or cardboard will compost – just make sure that it is mixed with sufficient 'green' material and kept moist. It can go in any composting or wormery system, scrunched or flat.

- 'Cardboard mould': you can even make a heap of just cardboard sheets and grass cuttings – an inch or two of grass, then a sheet of cardboard. Carry on sandwiching the two materials – you don't even have to rip up the cardboard! It makes a wonderful peat-like substance for use in seed and potting composts (see 'seed compost', page 92).

- Line compost heaps with it – especially home-made bins made from old wooden pallets. It stops material falling between the slats, and helps to insulate the heap.

- Sheets can be put down around perennial plants as a 'barrier mulch' (see page 86), which suppresses weeds. You can hide the cardboard with a layer of compost or soil, etc.

Carpet and carpet underfelt

Only pure, natural carpets and carpet underlay (wool, silk, jute, hessian, etc.) can be composted, or successfully used as mulches, A square of carpet on top of a compost heap is generally useful as insulation and moisture control. It's not vital for this compost cover piece to be natural, but be wary if using non-natural materials as a mulch because they can easily get incorporated into the soil and you will be pulling long warp threads out of your soil for years to come! Test a few threads of the carpet with a match: if they melt, they aren't natural! Also, be aware that although the weft of the carpet may be completely natural the long warp threads may well be of a man-made fibre.

Cartons

- Waxed cartons will eventually compost, but they take a long time. Many cartons and frozen-food boxes have a thin skin of plastic, which is a nuisance in the compost, although you can sieve it out.

- You can make a separate heap just for this kind of material – mix with grass cuttings. Beware, however: it takes a very long time to break down.

- Alternatively, these plasticised cartons make excellent flower pots: a 1-litre carton will support a tomato plant and you can even plant the whole thing out (you can remove it at the end of the season). Don't forget to cut drainage holes or remove the base.

Cat faeces *see Dog and cat faeces*

Cat litter (*see also Dog and cat faeces*)
Cat litter is compostable only if it is made from a natural product.

Cation exchange capacity (CEC) (*see also Colloids, Humus, Soil types*)
Clay soils and humus-rich soils both have high cation exchange capacity, which means that the molecules have a negative electrical charge, which attracts positively charged nutrients – cations – making them freely available to the plants. As a result these types of soils are the most fertile. The best way to build cation exchange capacity in the soil is by applying composted products and leafmould, and building up lasting humus by minimal tilling or no-dig cultivation.

Cations (see *also Cation exchange capacity, Humus, Soil types*)
Pronounced 'cat-iron', these are positively charged ions – very small particles held in the soil by the negatively charged clay and humus particles. Many minerals and nutrients are cations, including the important nutrients potassium, magnesium and calcium.

Charcoal (*see also Biochar, Activated charcoal, Humus*)
Charcoal is a fuel but you can add it, ground up, to soils as biochar. It behaves like humus in the soil, i.e. very stable, resistant to change and with a large surface area that holds water and nutrients. You might be able to get charcoal dust (or 'fines') from a charcoal maker.

Charcoal ash (*see also Wood ash, Biochar*)
It is fine to add this to your compost heap in small quantities.

Chemicals (*see also Aminopyralid, Clopyralid, Manure*)
Most modern agriculturally used chemicals will break down in the compost heap. I don't advocate using them, but if you are picking up materials to compost you might well be importing some chemical treatments inadvertently. The composting process is incredible in the way that it takes chemical compounds apart; however, some modern broadleaf herbicides have been resisting breakdown and are still active in some manure heaps – see *Manure* for more on this.

Chemical fertilisers
I'm an organic gardener and so I don't use chemical fertilisers. Chemical fertilisers have adverse effects on the soil food web; they can also often have a higher salt content than table salt, to which most plants cannot tolerate high exposure.

Chicken manure (*see also Activators*)
Use as a compost activator, but always mix manures up with 'brown' material to introduce air and carbon.

Chippers *see Shredders and chippers*

Cigarette butts
The filter tips on cigarettes are not biodegradable, but the rest of the cigarette will compost. Nicotine is highly toxic to wildlife, so cigarette ends should not be thrown into the environment (especially when lit), as some birds will pick them up and get poisoned.

Citrus fruit (*see also Fruit*)
I'm always being told that orange peel doesn't compost! But I've been doing it for years. Organic citrus is not sprayed with fungicides and pesticides and so the compost microorganisms do not have a hard time, but even non-organic citrus will eventually decompose. Half oranges and grapefruits are great for attracting slugs – pick them up in the morning and rinse in a bucket of water and put back again – the slugs will eat off any wax on the skin too, and then the halves are much easier to compost.

Clay *see Cations, Cation exchange capacity, Colloids, Soil types*

Clopyralid (*see also Aminopyralid, Manure*)
This is a chemical weedkiller that is extremely resistant to being broken down in the composting process.

Clothes *see Textiles*

Coal ash (*see also Additives, Charcoal ash, Wood ash*)
Although coal was formed from living organisms, this was at a time when our atmosphere was very different. Coal ash contains high levels of sulphur. Very small amounts will not be a problem – so if you have the odd piece of coal in a wood fire don't worry – but if you are burning coal all the time and have large amounts of ash to dispose of then it will poison the soil. (Wood and charcoal ash, however, are fine for composting.)

Coffee grounds
These are a good compost activator – get them from cafes or your canteen for composting if you can! If you have very large quantities you will have to find other

materials to mix with them, as with large quantities of most materials. Coffee grounds are also said to be a good slug/snail deterrent.

Colloids (*see also Adsorption, Cation exchange capacity, Humus, Soil types*)
Colloids are very small particles. (The word comes from the Greek for glue.) Clay soils are colloidal (and stick like glue!) and humus is too. Clay and humus have a negative charge; they adsorb positively charged ions (cations), which include many minerals and nutrients. Water has a polarity – it is composed of oxygen and hydrogen; the oxygen has a slight negative charge while the hydrogen has a slight positive charge – so the positive pole of the water molecule is attracted (adsorbed) by the colloidal particles of clay and humus.

Comfrey (*see also Activators*)

Comfrey, especially the hybrid varieties of Russian comfrey that Henry Doubleday devoted much of his life studying, is valuable both as a compost activator (being very high in nitrogen, with a 9:1 C:N ratio) and as a liquid feed. It is a vital part of any organic garden.

Comfrey is one of the highest natural sources of potassium, and is best used as a liquid, which you can make yourself, as follows.

- Chop the whole plant off at the base, preferably before it sends up flowering shoots (it will soon grow again!).

- Push the plant into a barrel with a tap on the bottom, and force it down with a spade to get as much in as possible.

- Put a weighted lid on top, and catch the liquid that comes off in a bucket. (You can use the same design as for a half-barrel wormery – see page 75). Add a small amount of water (or water and urine) to get the flow going. Some people tell you to immerse the whole plant but you get a very smelly liquid if you do.

- Water down the liquid (1 part liquid to 10 parts water) and use as a foliar feed – great for tomatoes and all fruit.

For more information see Garden Organic (www.gardenorganic.org.uk).

Community composting

Getting together with other people to make larger-scale composting systems can lead to a whole other world of activities. See Chapter 7 for more information.

Compost

Compost has two distinct meanings – one refers to the end product of the composting process, the other refers to what is more correctly described as 'growing medium', which may or may not contain any compost. It can be peat-, coir- or soil-based (see Chapter 6).

Compost extract (see also Worm casts)

This can be used as a foliar feed or on the roots of your plants. Use only really well-made compost or worm casts for this, i.e. nothing that has gone anaerobic or smells bad.

- Put 1-2 litres of worm casts in a large 50-litre bucket.

- Add about 30 litres of water and stir vigorously.

- I just stir around and use straight away – if you leave it in the bucket for too long the contents go anaerobic and smelly and you will kill the very micro-organisms you want. Other authorities say leave it to steep for one to two weeks, but I wouldn't advise that unless you are going to make compost tea (see opposite).

- Strain and dilute at least 1:10.

- Use as a foliar feed on your plants, but don't spray plants in full sun or you may scorch the leaves.

- For maximum effect add a drop of liquid soap (not detergent) and aim to coat leaves both above and below; or you can use as a drench around the plant.

Compost leachate (*see also Carbon piles*)

This is the dark liquid that is produced by compost heaps, which you will really notice only if your bin has a base to it. It can contain plant pathogens and so is best used as a nitrogen source for other compost piles – I add it to my sawdust/wood-chip piles, for instance, but you could just recycle it back through your compost heap. If your heap is producing a lot of liquid then add more absorbent material such as cardboard to soak it up.

Compost tea

Compost teas are made by steeping compost in water, adding microbial food sources, such as molasses and kelp powder, and bubbling air through the solution for 24-72 hours or so to keep the tea aerobic. You can use aquarium air bubbling devices; for a large bucket (about 50 litres) you will need up to three of these bubblers to make sure that the tea is kept aerobic. Larger systems can also be made or bought from specialist suppliers.

The tea must be used as soon as it is brewed and must not be allowed to go anaerobic. Compost teas multiply the beneficial microorganisms in your compost, and you can then apply the tea, after sieving out the larger particles, as a foliar spray or a root drench.

As with all foliar spraying, do not do this in bright sunshine or you can scorch the leaves. By covering the leaf surface of the plants with compost tea you are doing two things:

- You protect the plant and help plants to recover from attack from pathogens, moulds, etc. The tea overwhelms any pathogens by both the number and diversity of microorganisms.

- You feed the plant directly with soluble nutrients.

Root drenches help to do the same in the rhizosphere – the area of soil inhabited by the plant's roots.

Elaine Ingham is an authority on this area – see her website www.soilfoodweb. com. Also see www.attra.org/attra-pub/compost-tea-notes.html#compostteas.

Contaminants (*see also Bioremediation and Pathogens*)

People are naturally concerned that they are not contaminating their compost with any toxic polluting chemicals. Many of the foods we eat contain (or have been sprayed) with chemical pesticides and preservatives, and paper and cardboard will contain certain amounts of chlorine, boron and some chemicals from inks, although most inks nowadays are made from vegetable-based dyes.

The composting process itself is incredibly effective at dismantling complex, man-made, carbon-based chemicals, and different bacteria will eat a whole range of pollutant materials, including diesel and old tyres – although this doesn't mean you can chuck old tyres on to your compost heap! Contaminated soils can be processed by large specialised companies by bioremediation.

Cooked food

Do not put cooked food into either a dalek-type or an open garden bin such as a New Zealand box as it will attract rats and flies. However, it can go into several composting systems. For more details see Chapter 4, page 52 and Chapter 9, page 151.

Alternatively, having pets, especially dogs, is a great disposal route for most cooked foods.

Cooking oil and fat

Used cooking oil and fat cannot be composted in a small standard garden compost system, e.g. a 'dalek'. However, it can go into most other enclosed composting systems, such as the EM Bokashi system, tumbler compost bins, wormeries, digesters and Green Johanna bins (see Chapter 4); just mix with absorbent cardboard or paper before adding. If you are careful you can compost it in a larger garden compost heap, providing you don't add too much at a time. Just make a hole in your heap and pour it in, covering it over with vegetable matter afterwards.

You can also thin down oil with some paraffin and use it to coat a wooden compost bin, to help preserve it.

Cool composting (see also Wormeries)

You don't have to reach really high temperatures to make good compost, in fact most of the time most composters are making cool or slightly warm compost, and that's fine, as long as there is sufficient air flow and moisture. Generally, because we are adding relatively small amounts at a time, we are not generating and maintaining heat – especially in a small compost heap – but that's fine for the lower-temperature bacteria, the fungi and other micro- and macro-organisms, especially the worms, who like it cool. See Chapter 2 for more details.

Couch grass see Pernicious weeds, Turf

Dairy food (see also Food)

As with all cooked or animal-derived food waste, dairy produce can only be safely composted by a food waste composting system. All food stuffs have to be mixed with the appropriate materials to enable them to compost properly.

Dalek

This is the nickname given to the most common sort of mass-produced composters because of their similarity in shape to Dr Who's most famous adversaries. (See Chapter 4, page 41, for details of these composters).

Digester (Green Cone)

This is more of a waste disposal route in situ than a true composting system. You don't harvest any compost from a Green Cone, but they certainly enrich the soil wherever they are placed. (See Chapter 4, page 53, for details of these composters.)

Diseased plants

You need a well-managed, regularly turned, hot system to tackle diseased plants, which is why most gardening experts will tell you to burn them. However, if you can get your compost heap to the right temperature, the bacterial 'fire' of the heap is just as effective.

Composting is an amazing process: an astonishing number and variety of organisms are involved, and the heat generated can easily reach 60-70°C. Plant and animal pathogens, as well as weeds, are destroyed by the heat generated by the heap, and the hotter it gets, the more quickly they die.

Weed seeds and human and plant pathogens are generally killed during the first few days of hot composting, when the temperature is above 50°C. But even at just above 40°C, few will have survived after a month or so.

To ensure complete pathogen removal it's important to mature your compost. The warm, post-hot composting phase produces the 'hygienisers', i.e. the organisms, including worms, that attack pathogens.

Dog and cat faeces

These can contain parasitic worms that can cause blindness, and therefore it is generally not recommended that they are composted, especially when there are children around. However, a carefully made hot compost will destroy these pathogens; always cover them up in the heap or add to an 'in-vessel' system, which stops flies getting in (Worm city, see www.wormcity.co.uk, markets a wormery for pet poo).

If your council has a kerbside collection scheme for compostable materials, it will not be willing, quite understandably, to take products such as these because of all the possible health risks. Do not put them out for collection – and please don't throw plastic bags with animal faeces into hedges, or leave them dangling from trees – put them in the designated dog poo bins provided by the council. You can get biodegradable bags for your dog poo, but finding out about all the nuances of degradable, biodegradable and compostable bags is a bit of a minefield. Rebecca Hosking has done masses of work on this, leading to Modbury becoming Britain's first plastic-bag-free town – see www.plasticbagfree.com (information on biodegradable bags under 'Bag info'), and inform yourself as to these differences and why it is such a good idea to carry a cloth bag at all times.

There are now many manufacturers of biodegradable fully compostable bags, but do check very carefully to ensure that they are made from plant material and do say that they are compostable – if it just says 'degradable' then they are just made of plastic that falls apart.

Drinks cans

These cannot be composted. Recycle them at your local recycling centre.

Dryness

If you dig into your heap and find it dry and musty, don't dig any further. Soak it with water first so that you don't breathe in lots of spores from fungi, then dig it out and re-stack, mixing in plenty of 'green' matter (see 'Greens'). Cover up with plastic or carpet to retain moisture.

'Duvets'
Compost bin 'duvets' enable a small bin to maintain composting temperatures even during the winter; you can make them yourself or you can buy them for some types of compost bin (e.g. the Green Johanna).

Dynamic accumulators (see also Activators, Biodynamic compost)
Many plants (often our worst weeds, particularly those with deep tap roots) are 'dynamic accumulators' – they concentrate various minerals, bringing them up from deep in the soil where they become available to plants with shallower root systems. They also tend to grow in soils that are deficient in these minerals, so helping to balance the soil's nutrients. So if you have these as weeds in your soil, hoe them down and leave the roots in situ to cycle the nutrients, or use them in your compost – but first see *Pernicious weeds* for how to deal with such weeds.

All the plants used in the biodynamic compost preparations (see *Biodynamic compost*) are dynamic accumulators. Some of my favourite dynamic accumulators are comfrey, clover, dandelion, dock, stinging nettle and yarrow.

Earth (see also Loam stacks and long-term pernicious-weed stacks)
You don't want to put large amounts of earth into a compost heap. It's true that a light sprinkling can help introduce beneficial organisms, but earth is primarily composed of the weathered bedrock you happen to be on – and is about as useful and heavy as brick dust. So shake as much earth as possible off weeds in the normal composting system, and use the loam-stack system for really earthy lumps such as matted couch clumps.

Eggshells
The calcium in eggshells makes a useful additive to the heap, helping neutralise acid conditions in the heap and in the soil. But they will break down more rapidly if you crunch them up a bit as you put them in your kitchen caddy.

Eggshells are very popular with worms; the half shells make little refuges for them.

Fish (see also Meat and fish)
The Incas used to bury a fish under sweetcorn seeds to help fertilise the growing plant.

Fish can be composted in food-waste composting systems.

Flats
If you live in a flat or apartment and do not have access to any garden or outside space, you can still use a wormery to compost at least some of your kitchen waste (see page 63). You can also use a Bokashi system if you have somewhere to mature the compost.

Flies
You may well find that you get masses of tiny flies that fly up when you lift the lid of your bin. These will mostly be harmless fruit flies that are attracted by fruit. One way to control them is to leave the lid off the bin (or half off) for a while. This allows access for larger predatory beetles, which will set up home in your bin and will soon be feasting on fruit fly larvae. You can also wrap fruit waste in paper, or bury it in the heap and add the occasional sprinkling of garden lime. I use 'limestone flour', which you can buy as a mineral supplement for horses (see *Additives*) – don't be tempted to use fly spray!

You usually get a few flies around compost heaps, or may see maggots in your bin. Flies are a natural part of the ecosystem and a compost heap with plenty of predators in will keep down fly numbers, but if you get a lot then they are being attracted by something. Larger flies, such as blowflies, are attracted by meat, manures and cooked kitchen scraps, which is why you should make sure you use the correct type of composting system if you wish to compost these materials. (See Chapter 4, page 52.)

Be careful that you don't start infestations of flies in your kitchen caddy before you even get to the compost heap. Fruit flies in particular can multiply very quickly. Wrap fruit up in paper before you put it in the caddy or empty daily, especially in warm weather.

Food (*see also specific food item, e.g. Meat and fish, Vegetables, etc.*)
Books and leaflets on composting are always telling us to avoid cooked food waste and meat, fish and dairy in compost, but that is because this type of waste smells and attracts flies and vermin. However, if mixed with the right materials – structural woody materials to provide airflow and to allow liquids to percolate (see Chapters 2 and 3) – and/or put in the right systems (see Chapter 4), then all food waste can be composted without undue smell, flies or vermin. Also see Chapter 9 for more on composting food waste.

Food-waste composting systems
Systems for composting any food waste, including cooked food, meat, fish and dairy, are dealt with in Chapter 4. They all are designed to keep out most flies and vermin and either accelerate the composting system, ferment the food waste, digest it, or make it available as food for worms.

Fruit (*see also Additives*)
All fruit and its peel will compost, even citrus peel. Non-organic fruit is sprayed with preservatives, and citrus fruit is also treated with wax; both these factors slow down the composting process. If you make fruit juice, or have enormous quantities of fruit peel and pulp, make sure it is well mixed with other materials, especially absorbent 'brown' materials such as cardboard and paper, before adding to your compost system. It will be very acid, so add something alkaline (such as limestone flour).

Fruit flies *see Flies*

Fungi

Mushrooms and other fungi are fine in the compost heap. In fact, you may well see fruiting fungi of various types in your heap, and the white threads of their 'roots', called mycelium – this is quite natural. Your compost heap will be full of fungi, mostly microscopic, all doing a great job breaking down materials in your heap.

Garden waste (*see also Grass cuttings, Leaves and leafmould, Pernicious weeds, Shredders and chippers, Weeds*)

All plant material will compost – don't listen to anyone who says that you can't compost rhubarb or ivy, for example. However, some plants – particularly pernicious weeds – need to be handled with extreme care, and others do have irritating sap or hairs. These need treating with caution.

Woody garden prunings and branches will take a very long time to break down, unless they are shredded or chipped up first. You can use a lawn mower on some of this kind of material, but obviously not on thick branches!

Large pieces of wood are often better used as firewood or as wildlife refuges – many beetles depend on this kind of habitat. Some, like the stag's horn beetle, have become very rare because of people being over-zealous in clearing rotting lumps of wood from their gardens. Newts and toads also spend lots of time under rotting piles of wood, so why not find a place to make a wildlife pile, instead of trying to compost it all?

Giant hogweed (*see also Pernicious weeds*)

Giant hogweed is an impressive plant but if you brush against the plant in full sun you can get a nasty reaction and badly blistered skin. Do not let the plant set seed. Cut it down, but do not do this on a sunny day and make sure you cover your skin up. The sap is also irritating, so do not strim it either. You can chop it up and then it can be safely composted. The plant is controlled under section 14 of the Wildlife and Countryside Act 1981, which makes it an offence to plant it or cause it to grow in the wild.

Glass

This cannot be composted. If you do not have a kerbside collection, recycle it at your local recycling centre.

Grass cuttings (*see also Carbon-to-nitrogen ratio*)

Leave them on the lawn! As long as the grass is not too long it will not form a thatch on the top.

Although grass cuttings are really useful in composting systems, they can also be a headache, especially in large quantities, as they break down very quickly and you cannot stockpile them. You have to incorporate them straight away into your heap in very thin layers, which is where having a stockpile of cardboard or woody chippings comes in handy (see box, page 65). However, continually removing the grass cuttings from the lawn means they are not cycling their nutrients in situ, which gradually impoverishes the soil. This may be great for creating wildflower meadows, as they thrive on poor soils, but lush lawns need fertile soil to thrive.

Gravy *see Liquids and sauces*

Green Cone *see Digester*

Green Johanna

Green Johannas are large composters from Sweden, which come with a base plate and can compost pretty much anything. (See Chapter 4, page 54, for details.)

'Greens'

This is a generic term for anything rich in nitrogen; 'greens' usually contain a lot of water too. Greens are not always green, as all fresh fruit and vegetables are classed as 'greens' for the purpose of composting.

Hair

Do the hairdressers a favour and take your hair home to compost – all hair will compost, as it is rich in nitrogen, so all the pet hairs can go in too.

Hay

If you are lucky enough to be offered some hay bales, you can use them as building blocks for a super-insulated compost bin. Or you can break them apart and use them as a mulch around plants, or incorporate them into your compost heap. As with any 'brown' material in quantity, mix well with plenty of 'green' materials and make sure it is wet enough.

Himalayan balsam (*see also Giant hogweed, Pernicious weeds*)
This is an introduced species that is now naturalised in the UK. Although attractive, it can cause great problems due to its rapid colonisation of natural areas, out-competing native wild plants. It is controlled under section 14 of the Wildlife and Countryside Act 1981, which makes it an offence to plant it, or cause it to grow, in the wild. Control of this plant is the same as for giant hogweed but without the nasty sap – cut it down before it sets seed. Each plant can produce up to 800 seeds, which can be spread huge distances because of the explosive seedheads. The trouble is that people tend to grow it because it is an attractive and harmless plant, but then it gets out of control and spreads quickly, especially down waterways, where it thrives.

Hot heaps
For a compost heap to heat up and maintain a high temperature it needs to be at least a cubic metre in order to be self-insulating, or you have to have a well-insulated bin to maintain the composting temperature. To create a hot heap you need to assemble as many appropriate materials as possible and fill your bin in one go. (See Chapters 2 and 3 for more details).

Humanure composting
This word, a hybrid of 'human' and 'manure', was invented by Joe Jenkins, author of *The Humanure Handbook* – a highly recommended read. Composting human faeces and urine might not be the top of most people's agendas, but flushing it around the U bend and contaminating precious clean drinking water, which then has to be re-filtered and cleaned, is pretty crazy and a luxury most of the world cannot afford. The Chinese have been composting human wastes for at least 4,000 years – the classic book on this subject is F. H. King's *Farmers of Forty Centuries*, written in 1911 and still easily available. (See the Resources section for both books.)

I've been following the system that Joe goes into in great depth since 1992 and have never had any problems whatsoever. Visitors to our house are generally not aware that we are using a bucket system under the stairs. We don't have flies or smells, and the only slight problem is finding enough 'soak' (absorbent) materials to maintain this state. We generally use partially rotted sawdust and woodchip, which we have in a large pallet bin gently rotting away – they soak up the liquids really well. If we run out of this soak material we use compost or soil. Every few days the contents are emptied into my Scotty's Hot Box (but you could use a large compost heap – a New Zealand Box, for example) and covered with whatever is to hand; in the winter it could even be soil from the allotment, but usually it is some other actively composting material from my general garden compost bins (I use pallet bins) or any fresh green clippings, paper and card, etc.

I have a huge colony of worms in my Hot Box and digging it out is never unpleasant. The worms do an amazing job of finishing off the compost.

Humus (*see also Cation exchange capacity, Colloids, Lignins*)
What is humus? Much has been written about humus and there are many definitions

and discussions about what it really is.

- To the gardener humus is a loose colloquial term describing compost, leafmould or manure.

- To a soil scientist humus is the organic fraction of the soil comprising extremely small stable compounds, made of carbon, oxygen and hydrogen.

- Compost and manure, depending on how broken down they are, will also include nitrogen, phosphorus and other nutrients. When these nutrients have been taken up by the plants and the soil microbes, then what remains in the soil is humus.

- Humus acts like a catalyst in the soil, remaining largely unchanged and yet contributing enormously to the life in the soil by holding on to water and nutrient ions and releasing them to the plants when needed (see *Cation exchange capacity*).

- Humus is a colloidal substance, which means that it is 'sticky'. Colloids are very small particles but larger than molecules. Humus surrounds soil particles and creates a 'crumb' structure. Because humus does not contain nitrogen or phosphorus, i.e. major plant nutrients, it is not consumed by soil microbes and builds up in undisturbed soil.

Farmers and growers talk about getting their soil into 'good heart'. This primarily means building the humus content of their soils.

Hydrogen (*see also Acidity, Additives, Comfrey, pH*)
The amount of hydrogen in the soil determines the availability and solubility of all the elements in the soil.

Soils with high concentrations of hydrogen ions are acidic, and the elements iron, zinc, nitrogen and manganese are readily available. Conversely, the soluble elements calcium, potassium and magnesium are not readily available in acidic soils. Dolomite, which is a magnesium-rich limestone, is a good supplement for acidic soils, adding both calcium and magnesium, and growing comfrey is a way of adding the potassium.

Alkaline soils, which have low concentrations of hydrogen, are more difficult to treat. The addition of bulky organic matter, especially compost, is the easiest way for most of us to buffer the pH and to enable us to grow a wider range of plants that the soil would otherwise dictate.

Hygienisers
The name given to a group of soil organisms that kill pathogenic organisms left in maturing compost.

Indore compost
Yes I have spelt that correctly! I'm not suggesting you start making it indoors. Indore compost is the name given to the process that Sir Albert Howard developed in India in the 1920s. He made large compost heaps, ensuring a good mix of tough materials to provide airflow and soft materials to add the water. The very toughest materials were laid out in the road for passing buffalo carts to crush before adding to the mix. You can still get hold of his books – see Resources section.

Insects and invertebrates
The compost heap is a natural magnet for all kinds of wildlife, including insects and invertebrates, all doing a great job, so don't worry if your heap is heaving with life, unless you get an infestation (see under individual headings, e.g. *Flies*).

In-vessel composting (*see also Tumblers, Vertical composting units*)
'In-vessel' composting usually refers to large-scale, generally municipal, composters (see Chapter 9), but in fact any composting system where you can have a degree of control over the airflow and temperature, and that is sealed against vermin, is an in-vessel system.

Smaller 'in-vessel' systems are scaled down to household size – a tumbler is really a mini in-vessel composter. (See Chapter 4, page 60, for details of tumblers.)

Ivy *see Garden waste*

Japanese knotweed (*see also Giant hogweed, Pernicious weeds*)
This non-native species is extremely pernicious and difficult to kill. Like giant hogweed, it is controlled under section 14 of the Wildlife and Countryside Act 1981, which makes it an offence to plant it, or cause it to grow, in the wild. You can cut the top growth and compost it, but be really careful that you pick up every bit and do not cut into the crown. Attempt this only if you are a confident and experienced composter, and do it only on your own land. To be on the safe side, make a separate heap for knotweed just in case you start getting any regrowth. Don't use a strimmer on it – this will spread bits that can take root far and wide.

You can gradually bring knotweed under control by continually removing the top growth, but it will take many years. Herbicides also take a long time. If you are at all unsure about how to dispose of it, do not compost it or put it out for kerbside collection; instead dry it out and burn it.

Kitchen caddies (*see also Activated charcoal*)
There are now several types of kitchen caddy bins. Some have activated charcoal filters to help control smells; others are designed to be used with compostable starch bags and have perforated walls to allow for airflow. Unperforated bins can be lined with several thicknesses of paper (newspaper is fine), which will help absorb any liquids and keep the bin clean. However, the easiest way to avoid odours is to empty the caddy frequently into your compost bin.

Kitchen waste (*see also Food waste and specific food items, e.g. Meat and fish, Vegetables*)
When you are preparing vegetables for cooking, all the tops and tails and peelings can go into any garden compost bin. Similarly, any fruit waste – apple cores, orange and banana skins, etc. – can be added. However, although cooked food, meat and fish, cheese fats and grease can be composted, they need to go into one of the specialist sealed systems, e.g. a Green Johanna, as otherwise they may attract unwanted visitors. For more information see Chapter 4, page 52, and Chapter 9, page 151.

Leachate *see Compost leachate*

Leaching (*see also Adsorption, Anions, Cation exchange capacity, Cations, Humus, Soil types*)
Clay soils and humus-rich soils hold on to nutrients by adsorption (the molecules accumulate in a thin film on the surface of the clay or humus particles). Without humus in the soil constantly being topped up by bulky organic matter – compost, leafmould, manure and mulch – positively charged nutrients (cations) are quickly washed by rainfall (leached) out of the reach of the plant's roots.

Soils low in organic matter are low in the soil flora and fauna that ingest the negatively charged nutrients (anions), and so these nutrients are also quickly leached into the subsoil and out into the water table.

Leaves and leafmould
Small amounts of fresh and autumn leaves can be composted in a composting system, but since some gardens generate huge quantities of autumn leaves it is best to treat them as a separate system and make leafmould.

Leafmould is great stuff to have – especially if you want to make your own compost mixes for seeds, cuttings or potting (see Chapter 6). If you have, or can get, masses of autumn leaves, then make a special enclosure just for them (see Chapter 3, page 38).

Lids (*see also Moisture control, Flies*)
To have lids or not; that is the question. Home-made pallet bins or New Zealand boxes don't necessarily have them. Lids help with moisture control, obviously, but a tight-fitting lid keeps out predatory insects, which are great at controlling fly populations.

If you have lids, open up your bins from time to time when you are working in the garden to allow predatory insects access to the contents. I collect lids from old dustbins, etc., if I see them, to use on any home-made wormery systems, for instance. Covers made from old plastic feed sacks or pieces of carpet can be just as effective – or you could make your own from a piece of exterior plywood, for example.

Lignins (*see also Humus*)

These are very hard carbon compounds in woody materials that resist breaking down and form a major part of humus in the soil.

Lime (*see also Additives*)

If you use lime in composting systems it's important to use garden lime, not builders' lime, as builders' lime reacts with water and materials high in nitrogen, e.g. manures, which causes wasteful atmospheric release of the nitrogen. Also, using builders' lime is not pleasant as it can blow into your eyes, where it will react and sting like mad, as it heats up in contact with water. Use ground limestone or dolomite, which also has magnesium in it, in the garden, wormeries and compost heaps.

Limestone flour *see Additives, Lime*

Liquids and sauces

Gravy, custard, ketchup and the like are probably the most difficult type of materials to compost – but luckily you are not likely to have large volumes of these unless you are a caterer or are composting at work in a large canteen.

Adding *small* amounts of liquids to an actively composting system is fine, but if you have large amounts you need to combine it with coarse, dry woodchip to add air; paper or cardboard to add absorbency; and plenty of fresh 'green' material for nitrogen and living microbes. Ideally you should use an enclosed system, as recommended for cooked food waste (see Chapter 4).

Loam (*see also Loam stacks and long-term pernicious-weed stacks*)

Loam is a rich healthy soil with a good mix of sand, silt, clay and organic matter. Loam is really useful to have in growing media mixes. If you are not lucky enough to have a loam soil you can make your own equivalent by creating loam stacks.

Loam stacks and long-term pernicious-weed stacks (*see also Dynamic accumu-lators*)

If you have turf or a weed-infested grassy mix to dispose of and you want to make loam for your compost and potting mixes, use this simple method.

* Make a neat stack of the turfs and then cover up the whole heap with thick black plastic to exclude all light.

* Leave for a year.

* The result is a lovely rich loam.

With turfs infested with couch grass, or other weeds such as bindweed, ground elder, etc., leave the heap alone for about two years to be sure that all the weeds have died. Weed roots contain lots of valuable minerals so it's well worth doing this and safer than trying to compost them – a large earthy clod of weed can be insulated from the heat of even the hottest compost and survive to regrow.

Smaller amounts of turf can be treated in lightproof bags. Plastic sacks can let the light through, so if you use these cover them up to exclude the light.

Maggots (see also Flies, Lids)
Maggots are food to many creatures in the compost heap, so if you are adding foodstuffs with maggots or that will attract flies to lay their eggs, either make sure that you add it only to a very hot composting system or that predators such as beetles can get into the composter (by you leaving the lid off while you are working in the garden). Alternatively, you could try to find predatory beetles and introduce them.

Manure (see also Dog and cat faeces, Humanure composting, Mulches and barrier mulches, Zoo poo)
Fresh manures from herbivore animals are full of nitrogen and are excellent for turbo-boosting your compost. The poo from vegetarian small pets and their soiled bedding is fine in any system, but dog and cat faeces and litter (also check what the litter is made of – see Cat litter) can contain nasty pathogens, and parasitic worms. Poultry manure is strong stuff, so layer or mix it even more thinly than manure from horses, cows, donkeys, etc.

Fresh manure is wet, heavy and dense and is usually mixed with bedding, e.g. straw, hemp, wood shavings or shredded paper/cardboard. Mixed into your compost heap it needs similar treatment to grass cuttings: i.e. mix or layer well with anything that will help introduce air, absorb moisture and add carbon – depending of course on the quantity and type of bedding material already incorporated with the manure.

If you are buying a whole trailerload from a farm you have several options.

- Stack it, and cover for a year or so – depending on how broken down it is and how much bedding there is with it and of what type. Harder bedding materials such as wood shavings will take longer to break down.

- Spread it out on a barrier mulch of paper or card.

- Spread it direct on to land you want to clear for future cultivation (if you spread fresh manure around growing plants you may well kill them, owing to the very high levels of nitrogen that can scorch the stems of plants, and even if you don't the plants will put on masses of growth and then may often be attacked by pests. Some plants, e.g. comfrey, will be OK and even thrive, but it is not generally recommended. Rot the manure down first).

- Spread it direct on to land (or a barrier layer) and then cover with either a man-made cover (e.g. black polythene) or straw, hay, shreddings, chippings, etc. – see *No-dig* and *Sheet composting* for more on this.

You can then plant or sow directly into the various mulching systems with a careful choice of plants. You can broadcast various green manure seeds, e.g. mustard, buckwheat or clover, into the cover bedding layer. If the manure is very fresh you will be more limited as to what you can grow successfully.

Fresh or only partially broken down manure will also create leachate, so make sure this is not likely to get into any watercourses, where it can cause algal blooms, starve the water of oxygen and kill all manner of organisms. Covering to keep the rain off will largely stop this, either in a stack or in mulching systems.

Farmers often describe their manure as well rotted, but it often isn't. Make up your own mind – well-rotted manure should be like finished compost, i.e. you should be able to pick it up and it will not smell unpleasant or stick to your hands, but be nice and crumbly. Use only manure that is very well rotted if you are digging it into your soil.

Ask the farmer what has been sprayed on his grassland before you accept a load, as there are some chemicals (hormone-type weedkillers) that are approved for use on grassland to kill broadleaved weeds. The active ingredient is amino-pyralid, which is extremely persistent, staying active through the stock and right through the composting process, and it can kill susceptible plants even in minute concentrations. Another related extremely persistent chemical, clopyralid, is found in certain lawn weedkillers as well as in agricultural products, and can have similar results. Avoid them both if you possibly can.

Material *see Textiles*

Maturation and matured compost

The final stage of composting is the maturation phase. If it has been a hot heap it will gradually cool to the ambient temperature, the worms will move in and work over every last bit, and when there's nothing left for them they will move out to fresh pastures. This is a great reason to have two bins side by side. Alternatively, dig the top section of your compost out and harvest the lower levels, which should be fully matured.

How do you know when compost is fully matured? One test is to put a small amount in a plastic bag and seal it up. Leave for a few days and then open it up and smell it – if it has a lovely smell, as you would expect from dark, natural-woodland-floor leafmould, for instance, then it is mature. If it has developed an unpleasant whiff, then it is still not fully composted. So, if it looks like compost, smells like compost and feels like compost then it probably is compost! There has been whole a whole conference run on this topic, but a little common sense is all you need on a domestic level.

Meat and fish (see also Food, Kitchen waste)

Meat and fish scraps, whether raw or cooked, cannot be added to a normal garden compost bin as they can smell and attract flies and other larger unwanted visitors. These materials need to be composted within an enclosed composting or ferment-ing system, e.g. a wormery, EM Bokashi system, digester, tumbler compost bin, Green Johanna bin or other kind of in-vessel system. (See Chapter 4, pages 52-62 and Chapter 9, page 151.)

Metals

These cannot be composted; if you do not have a kerbside collection, recycle them at your local recycling centre.

Mice

A compost heap is a cosy hotel for a mouse family, often providing free food and a roof. So don't encourage them by putting food in a heap that is easily accessible to them. Keep them out by putting weldmesh under the bin and put the bin on slabs. If they are dead then you can compost them, but do it in a food waste composter because of the flies that will be attracted.

Milk see Dairy food

Mineralised compost

If your compost heap gets too hot, it can end up resembling charcoal rather than compost. This is not likely to happen to you with a home composting system, but I have seen it in large industrial-sized systems.

Really big compost heaps can get so hot that they ignite. This is why it is impor-tant not to bale and stack wet hay, as it starts to compost and because it's so self-insulating it can get so hot that it starts to burn.

Minerals *see Additives, Rock dust*

Moisture control (*see also Lids*)
It is difficult getting the moisture levels right all the way through the composting process. Hot composting releases a lot of moisture as vapour, which you can clearly see, especially on frosty mornings when the heap will be steaming away. A lid or cover can help to condense this vapour and recycle it into the heap. If too much vapour is released into the atmosphere it can dry the compost out too much.

On the other hand, if the heap is uncovered and it rains a lot then the compost can get too wet, so it's generally best to keep it covered. As the compost matures it's more important to keep the rain off as it becomes a lot denser and also more absorbent, so if possible cover it to keep the rain off but allow air to flow around, so that the compost can gradually dry out when it is mature. This is important if you want to sieve the finished product.

Montbretia (*see also Pernicious weeds*)
Montbretia is a very difficult weed to kill off. Put it in heavy-duty plastic sacks and exclude light. Leave for about two years, and then it can be safely composted.

Mulches and barrier mulches (*see also Manure, Sheet composting*)
Mulches are materials placed on the soil surface, or, in the case of barrier mulches, on uncultivated ground. They provide a wide range of benefits in different situations and times of the year, as follows.

* Moisture retention in the summer.

* Protection of the soil surface from heavy rainfall and erosion, particularly through the winter.

* Suppression of weeds, especially in the case of barrier mulches (see below).

* Help with pest prevention, e.g. cabbage root fly can be prevented by a mulch around the plant's stem (a card collar works too).

* Keeping crops clean – e.g. strawberries can be kept out of contact with the soil with a straw or bark mulch.

* Soil improvement – mulches of compost, wood and bark chips, manures, seaweed, wool and other organic matter provide nutrients and improve soil structure.

* Non-organic mulches, e.g. gravel, man-made membranes and even rocks, can help with moisture retention and weed control.

There are two types of barrier mulch:

- Short-term barriers, which use a compostable membrane such as cardboard or newspaper with a layer of natural mulch material, e.g. compost, manure, shreddings or bark chippings, on top. With a 4-6" layer of compost on top, seeds can be sown or plants established while the weeds are smothered underneath.

- Man-made membranes, such as black plastic sheeting. You can either lay this for several months to smother weeds, or you can cut slits in it and establish plants through the plastic. Potatoes are easy to grow this way and I've also done it with winter squashes, which soon sprawl all over the sheeting and cover it up.

Mycorrizhal fungi

Plants have evolved with microscopic fungi in the soil for millions of years, and most species of plants (probably as many as 95 per cent) have developed symbiotic relationships with them.

Mycorrizhal fungi can increase the surface-absorbing area of the roots of a plant up to 100 times, and hundreds of metres of fungal filaments can be present in just a teaspoonful of soil. Mycorrizhal fungi also enable plants to capture soil nutrients and minerals by releasing chemicals to dissolve them in the soil.

This fungal network is also important in water uptake and storage, and it improves soil structure by producing compounds that help create that crumb-like texture which improves porosity. However, mycorrhizal fungi are easily destroyed by chemical fertilisers and pesticides, as well as by soil compaction, over-cultivation or the removal of topsoil.

By applying compost and mulches, you help maintain and enrich the fungal populations in the soil. You can also buy mycorrhizal fungi to boost populations for specific habitats, e.g. lawns, golf courses, nurseries, etc.

Nappies

Disposable nappies are an environmental timebomb, as well as being unpleasant and offensive items in the dustbin. If buried in landfill sites, they are said to take centuries to break down. About 2 per cent of dustbin contents are made up of 'disposable' nappies – about 8 million a day.

There are now nappies on the market that are sold as 'compostable'. However, with a baby getting through six or more nappies a day you could end up with thousands of nappies in your compost bin! A keen composting mother I know has been investigating how well these nappies actually compost, and she has a huge pile, which are not composting. Like any composting system, you need the right mix, and to balance that flow of nappies would take a huge amount of green material.

If your council has a kerbside collection scheme for compostable materials, it will not want to take products such as 'compostable' nappies because of the offensive nature of the product and the health risk involved, and because of the vast volume of non-green waste that these nappies would present. Do not put 'compostable' nappies out for collection with other green compostable materials. Both 'compostable' and other disposable nappies must be put in the landfill bin.

The only really 'green' option is to not even consider using disposable nappies, whether they are compostable or not. Use reusable washable nappies; either buy and wash them yourself, or use a nappy laundry service.

The Women's Environmental Network makes the following startling points (see www.wen.org.uk/nappies).

- Home-laundered nappies could save parents around £500 on the cost of keeping a baby in nappies.

- You can kit out your baby in real nappies on the high street for under £50. This includes all the nappies and waterproof covers you need for the whole of your baby's nappy-wearing life. The same amount of money would only buy seven weeks' worth of disposables.

Nettles (*see also Activators, Dynamic accumulators, Pernicious weeds*)
Nettles are not difficult to find, and they make a really useful addition to your bin or heap. They will add bulk, moisture, nitrogen and plenty of beneficial minerals too. Their roots, however, need special care because they can easily regrow: see *Pernicious weeds* for how to deal with them.

Nettles can also be soaked in a barrel of water for a week or two to make an extract, which can be used as a feed.

New Zealand box
Originally designed in New Zealand, the main feature of a New Zealand box is that it is modular; usually two or more are used at any time, so that when one is full you can turn the compost into the next and then start again, using the contents of the second box on your garden when it is ready.

They have removable fronts in the form of planks, which slide up and off, making easy access for loading and emptying. They are generally at least a cubic metre in size. (See Chapter 4, page 44, for more details.)

Nitrogen *see Carbon-to-nitrogen ratio, Greens*

No-dig
If you are a no-dig gardener you become bit of a compostaholic and start viewing everything in terms of its composting potential or how well it could work as a mulch. If you become a really hardened addict you will probably have to start your own community composting project in order to get the supply of the quantities you need. For more about no-dig gardening see Chapter 6, page 82.

Nutrients
The major nutrients required by plants (nitrogen, phosphorus, potassium, magnesium, calcium, sulphur and silicon) can be divided into two basic groups, cations and

anions. (Of course there's also oxygen, hydrogen and carbon but for some reason these are not generally considered as plant nutrients although of course they are!)

• Cations are positively charged ions and are held by the negatively charged clay particles and humus. Most plant nutrients, with the exception of the anions listed below, are cations.

• Anions are negatively charged ions. The major anion nutrients are nitrogen, phosphorus and sulphur. Anions, in contrast to cations, are not held on to by humus or clay, but are held in the soil as the food of microorganisms, recycled as these organisms die or are consumed by other organisms.

Nuts *see Pips, nuts and stones*

Odour
All composting has an odour but it shouldn't be unpleasant: nasty pongs indicate that something is amiss in the process. The remedy is to get more air through the materials, by turning or tumbling, but most importantly by making the heap with enough structural twiggy materials in the first place to allow air and liquids to percolate through.

Oil *(see also Cooking oil and fat)*
Vegetable oils used in cooking can be composted in small quantities (see page 114), but new or used engine oil cannot be composted. Recycle it at your local recycling centre.

Paint *(see also Liquids and sauces)*
Natural paint, made entirely from natural materials, is compostable in any system, but must be well mixed with the appropriate materials. Do not try to compost any other types of paint!

Paper
Any scrunched-up paper can be composted. Most composting experts tell you not to put highly glossy magazine paper in (it is best recycled), but the odd bit is not going to hurt. Most inks used these days are benign, and the glossiness is mostly fine clay particles. Nearly all paper contains clay, which gives it a smoother surface, and clay is fine for compost heaps. (Although clay soils are hard to work, they can be extremely fertile).

Pathogens
Composting is incredible in the way that it purifies diseased matter, but you must treat it with respect. Wash your hands carefully after handling compost – especially if you have been more adventurous with what you compost.

If you make compost that heats up to 60°C or more, and turn it until it stops reheating (whether in a tumbler, by machine or with a hand fork), then that temperature will penetrate throughout the mass of the heap and kill any pathogens present.

If that wasn't enough, or if your compost hasn't reached such high temperatures, then the warm 'mesophilic' stage of composting has 'hygienisers' – organisms that produce antibiotics. During the final maturing of the compost, worms have been shown to kill any residual pathogenic material.

Pernicious weeds (*see also Loam stacks and long-term pernicious-weed stacks, Mulching, Weeds, and specific weeds, e.g. Japanese knotweed*)

I think of pernicious weeds primarily as those weeds that will grow from tiny fragments of root, for example, couch grass, ground elder and bindweed, but the term also applies to plants that have the capacity to monopolise though runners (e.g. buttercups, nettles and creeping thistle) or by seed (e.g. other thistles, dandelions and docks – pictured below).

All top growth of weeds can be cut and composted, but it is more problematic including parts of the crown of the plant or the roots, unless you are confident that you have a really hot heap that will cook them. If not, it's probably best to exclude them from your compost heap, and treat them separately.

- Put them in lightproof bags, or pile and stack and cover with heavy-duty black plastic sheeting and leave for 12-18 months (see also *Loam stacks and long-term pernicious-weed stacks*).

- Mulch the ground with heavy-duty black plastic, which will kill the weeds in situ given sufficient time. Or use cardboard; many weeds will survive and start to punch their way through, but these can then be hand dug and treated as above.

Alternatively, there are ways you can treat the roots and crowns in order to render them safe to add to your compost.

- Dry them out thoroughly, either on a wire frame outside or under cover if wet. Then you can add them to the compost. If they snap between your fingers they should be pretty well dead and safe enough to add, but if you are at all unsure and really don't want to spread your ground elder, nettles, monbretia, bindweed, couch grass, etc. then make a small bonfire of the dried-out roots – it's always best to have bonfire materials as dry as possible anyway as you don't want to create thick choking smoke.

• Drown the weeds in a barrel of water (you can put them in a hessian sack and weigh it down under the water). Leave them until they have rotted and gone very smelly, then they can be safely composted.

Under the Weeds Act 1959 the Secretary of State may serve an enforcement notice on the occupier of land on which injurious weeds are growing, requiring the occupier to take action to prevent the spread of injurious weeds. The Weeds Act specifies five injurious weeds: common ragwort, spear thistle, creeping or field thistle, broad leaved dock and curled dock See www.defra.gov.uk/farm/wildlife/weeds/index.htm for more information and www.ragwortfacts.com for ragwort; the latter site is interesting as it recommends letting the ragwort seed as the best control method, as long as there is no exposed soil around, as the plant dies after setting seed (though it might be a good idea to cover it with horticultural fleece to stop the seeds blowing away). Cutting doesn't kill the plant, and pulling leaves a ring of roots in the ground, which can lead to four or five ragwort plants growing where there was only one before.

Japanese knotweed, Himalayan balsam and giant hogweed are dealt with under the provisions of the Wildlife and Countryside Act 1981, which says that it's not illegal to have these species growing in your garden but that you should take every precaution to prevent their spread to wild land.

pH (see also Hydrogen)
This is measured on a scale from 0 to 14, with 7 being neutral. Numbers below 7 indicate acidity; the lower the number, the more acidic. Numbers above 7 indicate alkalinity; the higher the number, the more alkaline. Neutral soils, with a pH of 7, can grow the widest range of crops. Soils that are either more acidic or more alkaline can be 'buffered' by the addition of compost, which has the effect of neutralising either extreme.

Pips, nuts and stones
Pips, nuts and stones regularly germinate in my compost, and I've potted up lots of avocados and even an almond! If you leave them in the compost and turn the heap they will break down and become part of the compost.

Plant diseases
Many plant diseases can be suppressed by the application of compost and compost tea, including clubroot (which affects the cabbage family), white rot (which affects the onion family), brown rot (which affects potatoes) and many field crop diseases.

Plastic (*see also Starch bags*)
Avoid it – it will not compost, even if it says 'degradable'. Degradable just means that it breaks down into lots and lots of tiny pieces that persist in the food chain. Degradable plastic in the sea is eaten up by plankton feeders, which then store this plastic involuntarily in their bodies, so if we eat a plankton-eating fish we will then be eating that plastic too. That said, there are some fully biodegradable, compostable plastics. These are commonly made from potato and/or maize starch, and are used to line kitchen caddies amongst other things. However, unless you are 100-per-cent sure that your bag is compostable, leave it out of the compost heap.

Even the bags that are genuinely 100-per-cent compostable and biodegradable still seem to take an awfully long time to break down. I have been experimenting with some recently and they seem to come right through the composting process, but once out in the fresh air and daylight they do break down very rapidly. See www.plasticbagfree.com for information on biodegradable and compostable plastic bags.

Potatoes (*see also Pernicious weeds*)
Old potatoes and even bits of peel with the eyes in can grow in a compost heap, but you should spot any growing bits as you spread any compost. Pick these out and if possible add to a hot heap or treat as you would pernicious weeds. Unless, that is, you want potatoes volunteering themselves around your garden!

Processed food
Processed food contains a lot of salt and preservatives. Small amounts in a larger volume of material shouldn't be a problem, but if you are dealing with catering-sized amounts you will need to think carefully about what to do with this material. See Chapter 9 for more information.

Pulses
Both cooked and raw pulses will compost well.

Putrescible materials (*see also Kitchen caddies, Carbon-to-nitrogen ratio*)
These are materials with a high nitrogen and water content that start to break down rapidly and smell in warm conditions, e.g. your kitchen waste in its caddy in the kitchen. To reduce smells you can line your caddy with newspaper to absorb the liquid, and add cardboard and paper to your caddy to even up the carbon-to-nitrogen ratio even before your materials go into your composting system. Grass cuttings are also highly putrescible, which is why you must mix them immediately with some high-carbon materials.

Quick Return (QR) *see Activators*

Rats
Well, we all know that we are never far from a rat; however, we do not want to provide them with rat hotels and a free food source by putting all types of food

waste into an easily accessible compost bin. All the advice in this book about systems for cooked food, meat, fish and dairy waste is to enable you to compost this food waste without generating odour and attracting rats and flies, e.g. by rapidly hot composting in a tumbler, by fermenting in a Bokashi system, or by putting in a digester or other secure composter as described in Chapter 4. You are more likely to get rats if you provide easy accommodation for them, and the fashion for garden decking has done just that!

You must wash your hands thoroughly after handling compost, just in case a rat has been in your compost bin, because of the risk of Wiel's disease, which can enter the body through cuts or mucous membranes. However, canoeists are more likely to catch the disease than composters – about three canoeists a year contract the disease in this country.

So the sensible thing is not to handle compost if you have an exposed cut, but the chances are extremely slight that you will contract the disease, and I've never heard of any composting colleagues reporting any problems.

Raw food
Raw fruit and vegetables can be composted in any compost system. Any raw meat or fish needs to be composted within an enclosed composting or fermenting system. (See Chapter 4, pages 52-62.)

Rhubarb leaves
Contrary to popular belief, these are compostable. I wouldn't try eating them though, as they are very rich in oxalic acid.

Rock dust (see also Activators, Additives)
We know from the work of some of the pioneers of the organic movement that we need to have an intake of the full mineral spectrum. However, even if you are gardening organically and cycling the nutrients in your soil through your compost and back into the soil, if your soil is deficient in certain minerals then you cannot cycle those minerals around. (UK soils are generally deficient in selenium, for instance, and so fruit and vegetables grown in the UK will be deficient in this vital mineral, so it is a good idea to eat plenty of Brazil nuts, which are rich in selenium.) Rock dusts often contain a good selection of beneficial minerals and are great to add to your compost heap and soil, adding missing minerals and balancing the pH. Find out more at www.seercentre.org.uk.

Sand see Soil types

Sanitary towels (and tampons)
If your council has a kerbside collection scheme for compostable materials it will, quite understandably, not be willing to take products such as these because of all the possible serious health risks related to dealing with blood and other body fluids. Do not put them out for collection.

If you are a keen composter you can compost them yourself in your garden.

You can now buy sanitary towels that are biodegradable and fully compostable, but they must say 'compostable', not just 'degradable'. These can then be composted in an enclosed system such as a Green Johanna, but NOT in a normal 'dalek'-type bin. Organic cotton tampons can also be composted in the same way.

Sanitised compost
This is compost that has been composted to the point at which any human, animal and plant pathogens present have been reduced to acceptable levels. This generally refers to large-scale compost making that reaches temperatures of 60-70°C over days, which also cooks weed seeds as well as killing the pathogens.

Sawdust (see also Carbon-to-nitrogen ratio)
You can add sawdust very sparingly to your compost heap; it is very high in carbon (i.e. a 'brown' material), so it needs a lot of nitrogen and wetting from water and 'green' materials to get it composting.

Scotty's Hot Box
This should be called a warm box really. It came about because I asked the Worm Research Centre to make a cubic-metre-sized bin with a secure base and lid, because I couldn't find anything on the market that would be of the right size and secure enough to process food waste. They were meant particularly for schools and businesses, but some householders have also bought them. For more details see Chapter 9, page 164.

Seaweed (see also Additives)
It is worth collecting seaweed, as it is a wonderful additive for any heap, with an amazing complement of nutrients and trace elements. The best time to collect fresh seaweed is immediately after a storm, or directly from the sea itself. Don't collect seaweed from the beach at other times, as it is likely to have a high salt content from salt spray building up and becoming concentrated. Salt is toxic to soils and most plants, and it is difficult to wash the salt off without contaminating the soil and watercourses.

If you can't get any from the beach, it is worth buying a bag of seaweed meal and sprinkling some in your heap. Or you can buy seaweed extract; water it down to feed plants (as with comfrey juice), and put it on your heap as well.

If you live near the sea you can create no-dig gardens with seaweed. This is an ancient system practised in Ireland and Scotland called 'lazy beds', where they can cultivate on bare rock with just seaweed and some manure.

Seeds
Old seeds can be composted – I often find all kinds of seeds germinating in my compost. A quick turn, or more materials layered on top, will generally kill them off. However, don't put any in if they are treated with chemical dressings.

Sheet composting

Sheet composting is where materials are spread out directly on the soil; rather than alternating layers of high carbon with layers of high nitrogen in your compost bin, you alternate them in thin layers on the ground. So, for instance, partially rotted manure could be spread, then a layer of straw added to cover that and even a third layer of fresh grass cuttings could be put on top of that. The straw layer helps to regulate the moisture in the manure layer, keeping it damp, and also helps stop excessive leaching. The grass layer helps to keep the straw layer from drying out.

Using this method, ground can be cleared over the autumn and winter and by the spring the worms will have done much of the digging for you, but you could also incorporate some crops directly with this system, e.g. you could start in the spring and put potatoes on the manure layer. However, this is best done with more well-rotted manure.

Shellfish

These can be composted in an enclosed system and treated in the same way as meat, fish and cooked food.

Shells (from shellfish)

The calcium carbonate from the shells of shellfish will help neutralise acidic soil and prevent blossom-end rot in tomatoes (a calcium deficiency). It is also said to yield a better-tasting tomato.

If you have a shredder, it may be powerful enough to smash up shells from mussels, oysters, crabs, etc., or you can get your hammer out. Otherwise, bury them in your composter or wormery – the harder shells will take a very long time to break down, and will keep turning up in your garden, but will eventually disappear.

Shells (from eggs) *see Eggshells*

Shredders and chippers

Shredders crush or hammer materials, whereas chippers cut them up. They enable you to reduce heavy-duty prunings and other materials to a fraction of their bulk, and create a material with a massively increased surface area for composting. These chipped prunings are great for mixing with soft 'green' material; I always need hard chippings, particularly for composting cooked food waste.

If you have masses of chippings you can fill a whole bin with them and either gradually rot them down on their own (make sure you keep them moist – urine is very handy here!) or use them when you need something to layer with soft fresh stuff. Shredders range from the small, electric, almost silent, crushing type, to very noisy petrol- or diesel-powered chippers.

Silt *see Soil types*

Slow worms

You often find slow worms under, for instance, a carpet covering on a compost heap, or a piece of corrugated iron left on the ground near a compost pile. They look like snakes but are in fact legless lizards; they are quite harmless and are attracted by the rich pickings or insects and other invertebrates, such as slugs, thriving on your compost, and they like the warmth too. So encourage slow worms as natural pest controllers.

Slugs and snails
You get some quite spectacular-looking slugs attracted to compost heaps. Most slugs feast on wilted or decaying vegetation. The ones that go for living plants are small, orange and black or greyish in colour. You can just leave them alone on your compost heap, as they help to break down materials and are quite beneficial, as are snails.

Smells (see also 'Browns', Putrescible materials)
Compost heaps shouldn't smell unpleasant. If they do, then they need more 'brown', carbon-rich materials mixed in. You may have to dig out or turn the heap and mix in something dry and absorbent to open it up, e.g. cardboard, sawdust, wood chippings, dry weeds, paper, etc.

Snakes (see also Slow worms)
The most likely snake to visit your compost heap is the grass snake, which some-times lays eggs in the compost. Grass snakes vary in colouring quite a lot, from light green to almost black, but always have a yellow collar. The adder does not have this distinctive collar and has zig-zag markings on its back. All snakes and slow worms are protected species, so it's a real thrill to find them in the compost.

Soap
Soap is basically a fat mixed with a strong alkali – you can mix wood ashes with sheep lanolin and make soap, and both of these ingredients can be added to the compost pile. However, most soaps contain a long list of chemicals which I wouldn't like to add to my compost. Only the purest organic soap is really suitable, and I can't think why you would want to compost that!

Soil types (see also Colloids, Cation exchange capacity, Humus, Loam)
Soils are mostly based on the underlying rock type, and vary from coarse sands, with the largest particle size, through finer sands, silts and finally clays, with the smallest particle size. So the more particles per cubic millimetre of soil the more fertile the soil is.

A cubic millimetre of sand could be just one particle. A cubic millimetre of silt consists of around 1,000 particles. A cubic millimetre of clay contains around 1,000,000 particles.

- Sandy soils have particles between 0.05mm and 2mm. Sandy soils are the least fertile: water drains through them very readily and the small surface area cannot hold on to nutrients.

- Silt soils feel silky to the touch and consist of small inorganic soil particles measuring between 0.002mm and 0.05mm in diameter. Unlike clay particles they have an even diameter.

- Clay soils feel sticky. They consist of tiny particles, colloids, less than 0.002mm in diameter, shaped like flat discs, which stack together giving a very compact, dense soil with few air spaces. Adding bulky organic matter helps open up clay soils, providing air spaces and making clay soils the most fertile of all, with the highest cation exchange capacity.

- Loam soils contain a mixture of sand, silt and clay and are considered to be the most perfect of soil types. The clay gives high cation exchange capacity and the sand opens up the structure, allowing air to percolate and water to drain.

- Peat soils are generally very acidic as well as high in organic matter and low in available nutrients.

- Chalk soils are very alkaline and very low in available nutrients.

Whatever your soil type, the addition of compost will help, increasing water and nutrient retention in open sandy soils, allowing greater airflow in clay soils, adding nutrients to impoverished soils and helping to buffer the effect of pH in extremes of acidity and alkalinity. (See Chapter 1 for more on this.)

Soot (see also Wood ash)
Soot is sought after by onion growers, who hoe it in around their onions. It is rich in nitrogen and sulphur, and because it is black it helps the soil warm up.

Soup see Liquids and sauces

Stabilised compost
Compost that does not reheat after turning is 'stabilised' and can be used in the garden, especially as a mulch. I prefer to let the worms work through it first and then use the resulting well-matured compost.

Starch bags (see also Plastic)
Bags made from maize or potato starch are totally biodegradable and therefore compostable (do not confuse compostable with 'degradable'). Both kitchen and other green waste can be collected in these bags, allowing both bag and contents to be placed in the composting system or heap. However, unless you have large hot heaps the bags will not break down readily and you will have bits of plastic blowing around. However, they do seem to disappear pretty quickly when exposed to sunlight.

Stirrer

You may be given a device that looks like a harpoon with your compost bin. You plunge this into your compost and it aerates the compost as you pull it out, which is much easier than digging the whole heap out. However, I've never used one so I cannot personally vouch for their effectiveness.

Straw

You can use straw bales to make the sides of a wonderfully insulated compost heap. Alternatively, you can compost the straw by pulling the bales apart and using them as part of your 'browns' mix to add carbon to your pile. Straw can also be used as mulch around shrubs, fruit bushes, etc.

String (see also Textiles)

Natural string made from hemp, jute linen, etc. is compostable. Other string – such as baler twine, which is extremely useful for tying together pallets to make a quick container – is generally extremely tough and will not break down.

Tea bags

Not all tea bag material will compost, so if you are not sure whether the bag is compostable, it's best to break it open (easiest when dry), shake out the tea and discard the bag. You can add loose tea or organic tea bags, which have unbleached bags, to your heap, and can use these bags as a mulch too.

Tea leaves

You can compost tea leaves or use them as a mulch. Tea is high in nitrogen and is a good compost activator too.

Terra preta see Biochar

Textiles

You can compost any natural textiles, e.g. cotton, hemp, linen, silk, wool; if you are not sure, take a small piece of the material and try to burn it. Natural textiles tend to smoulder whereas man-made textiles tend to melt or burn.

Do not try to compost man-made or mixed textiles, e.g. polyester/cotton mix.

Thermometer

If you want to monitor your compost temperatures then a thermometer is vital. You can get expensive digital thermometers especially for compost, which have a metal spike you plunge into the centre of the heap – or you can make a hole with a bar and drop a thermometer in tied to a string.

If you just want a rough idea of temperature, thrust a metal bar into the heap and leave it for ten minutes or so then take it out. If you can hold the hottest part for only a second or two then you know it's pretty hot in there, probably 60°C plus.

Tins
These cannot be composted. If you do not have a kerbside collection, recycle them at your local recycling centre.

Tissues (*see also Pathogens*)
If your council has a kerbside collection scheme for compostable materials, it will, quite understandably, not be willing to take products such as these because of all the possible health risks related to dealing with body fluids. Do not put them out for collection.

Keen composters can compost used tissues, but if you are concerned about attracting vermin then don't put them in a standard garden compost bin, use a totally enclosed system such as a Green Johanna. However, the small amount of body fluids in used tissues is not very likely to attract unwanted visitors since the tissues will disintegrate very quickly when in contact with the wet materials in your compost.

Troubleshooting (*see also Additives, Air, Bioaerosols, Carbon-to-Nitrogen ratio, Dryness, Flies, Grass cuttings, Moisture content, Odour, Putrescible materials, Turning, Rats, Warmth, Water*)
Problems with compost generally come down to two things: either the heap is too wet and airless, or it's too dry and airy. Both problems are best solved by getting the mix as good as possible in the first place: refer to the mantra in Chapter 2.

Pulling apart a wet, smelly heap and mixing in absorbent and structural material is not the most pleasant job, and you will probably have to add more fresh green material as well to get the whole mass composting again.

Pulling apart a dry musty heap is also not to be recommended – the release of bioaerosols is potentially dangerous. A better solution is to soak it well, preferably with a high-nitrogen liquid such as manure that's been added to a barrel of water, or comfrey juice, etc.

Tumblers (*see also In-vessel composting, Turning*)
Tumblers take the hard work out of turning compost, which can be quite a chore. There are many different models, from balls that you can roll around your lawn or a barrel on a stand that flips over end to end, to larger ones with an axle running along the length, and insulated ones for year-round use.

Tumblers are ideal for composting all types of food waste as they are rodent-proof, and the insulated ones work through the winter. (See Chapter 4, page 60, for details of these composters. For more on food waste composting see Chapter 9 – this is mostly about large-scale food waste composting but much of the advice is pertinent on any scale.)

Turf (*See also Loam stacks and long-term pernicious-weed stacks*)
You can make a loam (good-quality garden soil) with turf – even from turf infested with weeds such as couch grass. Stack it neatly upside down, cover with heavy-duty black plastic and leave for a year or two. It will turn into wonderful crumbly

loam. Sieve before use, and use as ordinary garden soil.

Another option is to make turf chairs or a bench – just use the fresh turfs like bricks to create a living green bench.

Turning (see also Bioaerosols)

Turning compost heaps accelerates the process: it mixes up all the materials and allows fresh air in. You can monitor heaps when you turn them. Observe how moist the heap is and add more water or fresh green material (this is where materials such as grass cuttings are so useful) if it needs it. Alternatively, you can add more structural materials if too wet, to allow more airflow, and/or more absorbent materials, such as paper and cardboard, to soak up the excess moisture. Beware of turning musty heaps, which release a lot of bioaerosols.

Vacuum cleaner dust (see also Carpet and carpet underfelt)

Providing you do not have synthetic carpets (which will not compost and you cannot compost the dust from these), the contents of your vacuum cleaner can be easily composted by any compost system.

Vegetables (raw and cooked) see Food, Kitchen waste

Vertical composting units (VCUs)

These are a form of in-vessel composter. They look rather like silos – material is loaded at the top and works its way down, and gravity takes the hard work out of turning the material. This idea has been used in the Earthmaker composter (see www.earthmaker.co.uk), made in New Zealand but now on sale in the UK.

Warmth

Microbes need some warmth to be active – bacteria shut down below 6°C so the composting process will stop if the temperature drops below this. However, the composting process generates its own warmth, so as long as the mass of material is big enough or the container is well insulated it will keep warm.

Water

The main trick with composting is to get the mix right at the start. This means balancing the wet and the dry materials – the 'greens' and the 'browns'. If this is roughly right, the environment will be right for all the organisms that drive the compost system.

Compost systems need water, but they mustn't become waterlogged. The water must not fill up all the air spaces – it must be either absorbed (preferably) or allowed to drain away, otherwise everything drowns and it really starts to smell! If this happens you will have to dig it all out and mix with absorbent and free-draining high-carbon materials, like cardboard and wood chippings. This is why it is vital to drain totally enclosed systems such as wormeries on a regular basis.

- If the heap is too dry, many of the organisms just die or go away, and the compost stops working. If this happens you will need to add some water.

- If the heap is too wet (more often the problem), just make sure you add plenty of absorbent paper and cardboard.

Weed roots
Weed roots contain lots of valuable minerals, so it's a great shame to waste the roots of weeds. You can use them as follows.

- Dry them out in the sun for a few days before composting, but ensure the attached plant doesn't go to seed.

- For very earthy weed clumps such as couch grass, make a neat stack of the earthy clods, then cover up the whole heap with thick black plastic to exclude all light. Leave for about two years to be sure that all the weeds have died, and the result will be a lovely rich loam. Smaller amounts can be treated in light-proof bags.

- Drown them to release their minerals. They can either be put in a hessian sack and weighed down in a barrel of water, or simply put into a barrel of water with a cover on it. After a few weeks, the whole lot will rot and smell awful – so do it well away from human habitation! The smelly water can be used on plants (the smell will go away very quickly), and the plant remains can now be safely composted.

Weeds (*see also Dynamic accumulators, Loam stacks and long-term pernicious-weed stacks, Pernicious weeds, Turf, and individual weeds, e.g. Japanese knotweed*)
Weeds are great to add to compost heaps as long as they are not seeding profusely, and you have to be very careful what you do with the perennial pernicious weeds (see *Pernicious weeds*). Indeed, some require special treatment and it is illegal even to move them from your property.

Weeds tend to be wet and sappy, so try to mix them with some 'brown' material and always remove as much soil as you can from them, as this helps them to compost more readily – you don't want too much soil in a compost heap.

Weeds can be valuable in the compost, as many are 'dynamic accumulators', which means that they have the ability to concentrate minerals that are in low concentrations in the soil, thus making them more readily available for other plants. Some of them do this by having very deep roots, which bring up the minerals that are out of the reach of other plants, so don't burn them – just treat them with respect, as described above, in *Weed roots*.
Weed facts:

- Plants die without light.

- Most plants die without water, so dry them out on a wire frame – beware of bulbs and corms, though, such as montbretia, which is difficult to kill off.

- Most plants will 'drown' in water.

- Weeds are hardy, and can go to seed even after being pulled out the ground, or re-root if left on a damp soil.

- Fly tipping is illegal and causes the spread of invasive weeds.

Wetness *see Water*

Why make compost? (*see also Chapter 1*)
This is the really important stuff, so I've included it here in the A–Z for easy reference.

- By making compost you are multiplying beneficial microbes, which replenish and feed the microbial activity in your soil, and the microbes in turn help feed your plants. In other words, compost feeds your soil, which feeds your plants.

- The soil microbes not only help feed your plants, they also help to protect them from pests and diseases.

- Compost opens up clay soils and improves the water-holding capacity of free-draining sandy soils.

- Compost 'buffers' the extremes of acidity and alkalinity in a soil, meaning you can grow a wider range of plants on your soil.

- Much of what we are currently wasting was once living material, whether that is cardboard, paper, fruit and vegetable peelings, other food waste or garden prunings, clippings, weeds and so on.

- Compost saves you money, in that you don't have to go out and buy chemical fertilisers, and you should find that with the resulting healthier plants you don't have to use any toxic chemical pesticides.

- You also won't have to go out and buy composts, as you can make your own soil improver, potting composts and more.

- Why give all your potentially compostable material away to the council? Even if it is going to compost it you still won't get the benefits of the product. And if it's destined for landfill then by composting at home you can stop your dustbin smelling and save all that material from being buried or sent up an incinerator flue.

- Compost sequesters carbon – it locks up carbon in the soil rather than releasing into the atmosphere (see *Biochar*).

- Making compost is ridiculously easy; it's satisfying and fun, once you get hooked!

Windrows (*see also Woody materials*)
A windrow is just a pile extended sideways to form a long heap, which can be turned by a mechanical 'windrow turner'.

Gardeners with a lot of material might well make a windrow, particularly of woodier material, and biodynamic gardeners favour this shape of compost pile, but made with a mix of materials and left without turning.

Wood ash (*see also Additives*)
This is fine to add to a compost heap a little at a time – it adds valuable potash, calcium and phosphorus – although adding too much at any one time will result in a nasty sludge.

Woodlice
Woodlice are naturally found in compost heaps and are just one of the many species benefiting from a free food source and helping break down your materials into compost. However, lots of woodlice in your compost heap indicates that your compost is too dry, so give it some water.

Woody materials (*see also Windrows*)
Lots of people seem to get it into their heads that they shouldn't put woody material into the compost because it will 'rob nitrogen'. They have a point – if it is dug into the soil it will continue to need nitrogen to help it break down. But woody materials are vital in the compost heap to add structure and create airways. Of course you

have to get things in proportion – you can't go chucking great big branches into a dalek bin. Woody stuff either has to be shredded up before adding to your compost heap, or other strategies have to be devised for it, as follows.

- *Wildlife heaps.* If you have space, make neat piles of woody materials – these then become refuges for all kinds of creatures, from beetles to newts.

- *Long-term piles.* You can make woody piles very high. Try to chop bigger branches down a bit and fill and pack the spaces as neatly as possible – you can include soil, smaller materials, leaves and other green materials to fill up as much air space as possible. You need to leave these for at least two years and even then they will be only partially broken down. Get up on them and stomp them down; water them and they will go more quickly. If you have a lot of material you may want to extend the pile sideways into a windrow.

- *Supports.* Save some long branches for beanpoles and smaller sticks as supports for all kinds of plants, including peas of course, but also herbaceous flowering plants.

Wool *see Mulches and barrier mulches, Textiles*

Wormeries (*see also Worms* and *Worm casts*)
The opposite of hot composting, as worms like it really cool. Wormeries complete the range of options we have to make good compost, and make the very best compost, in the form of worm casts. (See Chapter 5 for information on wormeries.)

Worm casts (*see also Compost extract, Wormeries*)
Worm casts (or worm poo) are the most wonderful soil-conditioning material. A little goes a long way, and you can make it go even further by mixing with water and making an extract – see *Compost extract*. (See Chapter 6, page 88, for more information.)

Worms (*see also Wormeries*)
Worms should invade a healthy heap. There are several sorts; the first three are commonly found in wormeries.

- *Eisenia foetida*, 'tiger worms' (pictured opposite), which are red with yellow stripes.

- *Dendrobaena* and other *Eisenia* species – other types of red manure worms.

- *Enchytraeids*, small white threadworms (or pot worms).

- *Lumbricus terrestris*, the large mauve garden earthworm, although this appears only occasionally – it is usually in the soil or your leafmould piles.

These worms emerge from their burrows on wet, warm summer nights and, with their tails still in the burrow, scout around for organic matter to pull down into the ground. If you go out with a torch you can hear the slurping sound of them pulling themselves back into their burrows at speed when you shine a light on them.

Worms live in cool, moist conditions, and will burrow away from any hot composting that may be going on. (For more information see Chapter 5.)

Yarrow *see Dynamic accumulators*

Yoghurt *see Dairy food*

Zoo poo
Paignton Zoo sells 'Zoo Poo' made from elephant, rhinoceros and other herbivorous animals' poo. This is a great way for you to support the zoo and to get some great compost too. It is available across the south west and now in south-east England too – maybe other zoos will start to catch on to this potential income source. See www.ecosci.co.uk/zoopoo.php.

PART THREE

CHAPTER 9

COMPOSTING FOOD WASTE ON A LARGE SCALE

Composting food waste, especially cooked food, dairy products, fish and meat needs special consideration. If large quantities are being generated it becomes even more important to ensure that a robust system is in place before composting operations begin.

The technology for composting food waste safely has been developed to include all situations, from the householder level right up to business and institution level, and even beyond, although this book is not concerned with very large municipal-level composting systems.

While this chapter is really for anyone who wants to set up a composting system at their workplace, much of the advice is applicable to any scale of food-waste composting, from the household scale upwards.

Why do it?

Food waste has reached ridiculous levels in the UK. The Waste and Resource Action Programme (WRAP) estimates that we throw a third of the food we buy in the bin and that a third of all material ending up in dustbins is food waste; much of this food would have been perfectly edible.

Planning our shopping and using up leftovers will help, but nevertheless there will always be some food waste to compost, even if it is just the peelings, tailings, tea bags, eggshells and so on from the kitchen. This is not difficult to do on a household level, and I hope the book will encourage you to compost this material at home, but when you start to contemplate the scale and type of food waste coming out of cafes, restaurants and canteens in schools, factories, hotels, prisons, hospitals and other institutions, you have a very different situation to deal with.

Institutions are, rightly, wary of food waste composting. They have read that it cannot be done; that it will attract rats, flies and other problems; that it will smell and ooze horrid liquids and is generally a bad idea. In fact, anything that recently lived, and that includes mashed potato, beef burgers, gravy and custard, can all be composted; you just have to know how to do it.

Many local authorities now collect food waste for composting, and this is governed by extremely strict legislation, brought in during the big foot-and-mouth outbreak of 2001. But this legislation is mostly concerned with what happens to waste food when it is transported to a centralised composting plant, and does not cover 'in situ' food-waste composting. This leaves many places where the carefully considered composting of food waste can be carried out. Rather than having bins of smelly mixed waste attracting all kinds of unwanted visitors and needing regular costly collections, it can be a way of avoiding those problems and making wonderfully important compost to restore our depleted soils. Many schools, prisons, National Trust properties, rural hotels and B&Bs are now composting food waste, and the potential to do more is enormous.

Rising trade-waste collection charges for businesses, the legislation outlawing biodegradable waste from landfill, the rising cost of fuel and food, and the potential to save money by creating compost that can be sold are all factors that are making organisations and businesses consider composting.

How it works

There are two main categories of food waste coming from a kitchen.

- The first consists of discarded raw materials, mostly from preparing vegetables and fruit, e.g. peelings, onion skins, pea and bean pods, tops and tails, trimmings and so on. You can include in this category all kinds of other things that end up in the normal kitchen caddy, e.g. tea leaves and bags, coffee grounds, kitchen towels, dead flowers, and unused wrinkled or mouldy vegetables and fruit.

- The second category consists of left-overs, unserved foods, plate scrapings, raw meat, fish and dairy trimmings, shells from seafood, used oil, etc.

All of this material can be composted in the systems described in this chapter.

Composting cooked food needs more care as it is dense and heavy and devoid of microbial life. It needs to be mixed with roughly equal parts of dry woodchip/ sawdust and fresh raw food waste – the discarded material when preparing vegetables and fruit in the kitchen, which is called 'prep' in the trade (or you could use fresh green garden clippings if short on fresh prep).

Food wastes are 'putrescible', i.e. they are wet and nitrogen-rich and tend to start breaking down and warming up quite quickly, sometimes even when still in the caddy in the kitchen, and then start to smell and ooze liquids, especially in the summer; worse, they then attract flies. To avoid this, empty the caddy daily and mix with dry woodchip and/or sawdust, and get the material as quickly as possible through the hot, volatile, stage of composting.

Getting the mix right from the start is really important with food-waste composting. You really cannot leave stuff lying around in buckets going all smelly and anaerobic – it makes it much more difficult to start composting it aerobically.

All food-waste composting that includes materials from the second category of waste, especially large-scale systems, needs some form of 'in-vessel', or sealed, container. In-vessel machines are designed to be vermin-proof and as fly-proof as possible, and to be used in places where large amounts of food waste are being produced on a regular basis – they take the material rapidly through the hot stage of the composting process.

The Bokashi system

An alternative to hot composting and to having smelly food waste hanging around is to use the Bokashi system. Bokashi systems are generally used by householders on a small scale, as described in Chapter 4. The system *can* be scaled up using large containers such as wheelie bins, but this generally becomes rather unwieldy. More often, Bokashi is used as a way of controlling odours where caddies are left out for a weekly collection round. A small caddy containing the Bokashi mix is used in the kitchen, and emptied into a larger bin outside the front door of the flat or house; the handles on the larger bins also lock the lid down, which stops dogs, for instance, flipping them open. (Separating out food waste for collection has stopped rat infestations and odour problems on estates in London where this system has been pioneered by the community projects involved. See Chapter 7, page 96.) The food waste then goes into one of the hot composting systems such as the Rocket and Big Hanna, described on page 156.

Hot composting

Whether you are composting food waste at home with a small tumbler or using a commercial composter costing many thousands of pounds, the technique of hot composting food waste is basically the same.

- Firstly it needs to get hot and cooking for a good period of time, after which the material will be 'sanitised', i.e. any pathogens will have been killed.

- It takes less time to kill pathogens at higher temperatures, from minutes or hours at the highest temperatures of 60-70°C to days or weeks at lower temperatures.

- In-vessel composters vary enormously, but generally materials are retained for at least two weeks, after which time they should not reheat, however much they are agitated to introduce more air.

- For operators that collect and transport food waste for processing there is strict legislation governing this time and temperature combination. For 'in-situ' operations, this legislation does not apply, but it's still desirable to get the compost hot as this means it breaks down more quickly and you can process more material.

- After the sanitisation period of composting the material ideally goes through a longer maturation phase. For the scale of operations covered in this chapter, the material will need to be stored in relatively secure maturation units where worms will be the main organisms finishing the process. In very large municipal-scale operations this phase will consist of windrows on concrete pads outside, which are turned regularly.

Tips for food-waste composting

- Get all materials composting as soon as possible.

- Get the mix right – a simple rule of thumb is: one-third cooked food, one-third fresh peelings, etc. and one-third dry woodchip/sawdust. Because materials are so variable with regard to moisture and air content you may have to play around with these proportions to find what works best for you.

- The dry carbon-rich ('brown') fraction is also variable – ideally a mixture of particle size, from sawdust to large wood chippings.

- Adding too much cardboard to these systems is not a good idea as it tends to ball up in a tumbler and clog up other systems. Small amounts are fine; just don't use this stage as a main way of recycling cardboard or paper. However, if you can get hold of cardboard dust it is excellent to mix in as it helps boost the pH. (You can add more paper and cardboard to the maturation stage though.)

- Add a bucket or two of compost when you first load the com-poster, preferably from a food-waste composting system, and the microorganisms will kick-start the process.

- Loads of heat is produced when you get it right, and so the volume of the contents drops dramatically, as much of the volume of the material is water and this is released as vapour, so you shouldn't need absorbent materials once you get the hang of it.

- You can recycle the woodchip by sieving the contents into a maturation bin; that way you also get to cycle the microorgan-isms and build up the right ones for your system. The partially composted wood chippings also will now have a higher pH and will help to balance the usually rather acid food waste, helping it to compost more readily.

Systems for food-waste composting on a large scale

In-vessel systems, as well as being vermin-proof and fly-proof, also offer at least some degree of control over airflow, leachate and temperature. These systems are ideal for food waste as they mix and help to aerate the material. After quite a short period of time, even a day or two, the material changes in composition. It rapidly heats up and reaches temperatures of 60-70°C, it also changes visually from being full of colour (it is called 'fruit salad' in the business), to a more even brown colour.

These in-vessel systems can be categorised in two ways.

- 'Continuous throughput' systems, where materials can be added on a regular basis (usually daily) and material taken out regularly at the other end of the machine (e.g. Big Hanna, Rocket, Jora 5100, Ridan, vertical composting units).

- 'Batch' systems, i.e. a container is filled, either in one go or over a period of time, and then all that material is taken out, usually after 'sanitisation', to be matured (e.g. Jora 125, 270 and 400, Scotspin, static pile).

There are three basic different types of system, some of which are batch systems and some of which are continuous throughput.

- Rotating drums to tumble the materials.

- Turning mechanisms to stir and mix up the materials. This includes vertical composters, which use gravity to mix the contents.

- Static-pile systems, where air is blown or sucked through the materials.

These systems 'sanitise' (see A–Z Guide) the materials and kill weed seeds.

See the Resources section for information on suppliers of the composting systems described in this chapter. The Compost Doctors have been using most of the systems described here, plus other home-made and innovative systems, and are a good source of advice.

Tumbling or rotating systems

Nearly all the tumbling or rotating systems described here are batch systems. The exception is the Big Hanna, which is an electrically powered rotating drum that you load at one end and harvest from the other end, which makes it a continuous throughput system.

Small hand-powered tumblers

How it works

These systems, such as the Jora 125, 270 and 400 and the Scotspin, are ideal for food waste because they are insulated (other, non-insulated tumblers will also work – but only efficiently when the weather is warm).

If you tumble daily you can maintain high temperatures, especially if you keep feeding your compost with fresh waste; sometimes it seems as though you can never fill the chamber, and of course you must leave some space or it will not tumble effectively. Don't forget that you must get the mix right (see 'Tips for food-waste composting' box, page 153). When you have nearly filled the tumbler, stop adding more fresh material but keep tumbling. The temperature will start to fall off after a while without fresh material being added.

The Jora manufacturers claim that you can put about 20 kilos a week into the Jora 270, but that is in order to produce completely finished compost ready to go on the garden. However, if you do not wait for the compost to mature in a tumbler, you can put at least three times the recommended amount through the system. Although these systems are great at the first hot and warm phases of composting, and the manufacturers all claim that they produce finished compost, in fact the last maturation phase of composting cannot be hurried and I think you really need the worms to finish off the process.

So, I recommend using your in-vessel composter to do the first warm and hot stages of composting, then the material will be sufficiently degraded that rats are not interested in it. I've found that rats are likely to expend a lot of energy in breaking in to a compost system only if there is fresh food to be had; they are not interested after two weeks or so of hot composting in an in-vessel system, and so at this stage you can move the compost to a secure, but not necessarily completely rodent-proof, unit. The Scotty's Hot Box (see page 164) is ideal for this as it has a large capacity and is a challenge for rodents to break into, but you could make a secure maturation bay out of, for instance, concrete blocks on a solid base with a secure lid, or use a New Zealand box that is rat-proofed with weldmesh (see 'Maturation units', page 163).

Note that the Jora systems arrive flat-packed and need to be assembled, whereas the Scotspin arrives assembled and just needs putting on its stand.

Cost

Jora 125: £299.
Jora 270: £389.
Jora 400: £900.
Scotspin: £600.

Where to get one

Jora in the UK are available from Smartsoil (www.smartsoil.co.uk). Scotspins are available from the Worm Research Centre (www.wormresearchcentre.co.uk) and Proper Job Ltd (www.proper-job.org).

Pros of small tumblers

- Insulated.
- Accessible.
- Accelerate the hot phase of the composting process.

Cons of small tumblers

- Hand-operated drums get very heavy to turn when getting full.
- Hand-operated models need turning regularly.
- If components, such as clips, fail to operate properly then the contents can spill out.

Large powered tumblers (e.g. Big Hanna)

The Big Hanna is the only example of a powered throughput tumbler that is of a suitable size for institutional use, although there are much bigger continuous throughput tumblers that are used on a municipal scale.

How it works

Food waste is added through a hatch at the front of the composter and an equal volume of pelletised sawdust or dry woodchip is added at the same time. Air is sucked through the machine and generally through a biofilter to remove odours. As fresh material is added it displaces the material inside so that it moves along the composter. This means that more than the recommended amounts can be put through, and then matured outside the machine, as with the small tumbler systems.

The Big Hanna comes in a variety of sizes, from the T40, which can process 100 kilos per week, to the T240, which can process 1,200 kilos per week.

Cost

The smallest model of Big Hanna costs from £8,000. (Prices will vary from site to site depending on power supply and other site-specific considerations.)

Where to get one

Big Hanna (www.bighanna.co.uk).

Top: the Big Hanna at Okehampton Community College.
Bottom: the author inspecting the Big Hanna.

Pros of Big Hanna

- Can compost large amounts of food waste quickly without flies, smell or rodent problems.

- Largely automated.

- Continuous throughput.

- Great at mixing and getting compost through the thermophilic 'hot phase' of composting.

Cons of Big Hanna

- Price (although machines should pay for themselves in time).

- Need for electrical supply – often three-phase.

- Need for a building to house the machine.

- Often need for additional equipment – de-watering machines, macerators (the manufacturers recommend shredding or grinding the food waste first so that it will compost more readily, and some systems require water to do this; however, then the material is too wet and so it has to be centrifuged to remove most of the water – the liquid fraction goes down the drain).

- Often need to have additives to control odours and control conditions inside.

- Need to buy in pelletised sawdust, or woodchips to mix with the food waste.

- Can take quite a time for those using it to get it right.

Turning mechanism systems

How it works

These generally have paddles inside that turn the material and gradually push it from one end of the composter to the other. Pelletised sawdust or dry woodchip-pings are also added to create the right mix, as with all the other systems. Examples are the Rocket, Jora 5100 and Ridan.

Electrically powered turning mechanism models

The Rocket needs to be housed and connected to an electricity supply, generally three-phase; it has a single chamber and paddles to turn and move the materials along inside.

The Jora 5100 needs to be housed and connected to an electricity supply, generally three-phase; it has two chambers and the second chamber is used to mature the compost.

Cost

From £8,000 for the smallest Rocket up to over £100,000 for much larger bespoke machines.

Pros of electrically powered turning mechanism models

- Can compost large amounts of food waste quickly without flies, smell or rodent problems.

- Largely automated.

- Continuous throughput.

- Great at mixing and getting compost through the thermophilic 'hot phase' of composting.

Cons of electrically powered turning mechanism models

- Price (although machines should pay for themselves in time).

- Need for electrical supply – often three-phase.

- Need for a building to house the machine.

- Often need for additional equipment – de-watering machines, macerators (the manufacturers recommend shredding or grinding the food waste first so that it will compost more readily, and some systems require water to do this; however, then the material is too wet and so it has to be centrifuged to remove most of the water – the liquid fraction goes down the drain.)

- Often need to have additives to control odours and control conditions inside.

- Need to buy in pelletised sawdust or woodchip to mix with the food waste.

- Can take quite a time for those using it to get it right.

Where to get one
Joras are available from Smartsoil (www.smartsoil.co.uk). Rockets are available from Accelerated Compost (www.quickcompost.co.uk).

Hand-powered turning mechanism models

There is a hand-powered machine called the Ridan, named after Richard (Gedge) and Dan (Welburn), who developed it. It's basically an insulated pipe with an axle running along its length with paddles along it, which you turn using a large wheel. Material is put in through a hatch at one end and exits at the far end underneath.

This composter will compost 40 litres* of cooked food waste, plus 40 litres of raw peelings, etc. and 40 litres of dry woodchip per day. (This is equivalent to the throughput of the smaller Rockets and Big Hannas.) The materials are put in and mixed around with the turning wheel, and about 30 litres per day are harvested at the same time. The biggest woodchips are generally sieved off to re-use and the remaining materials are added to a maturation unit to finish composting.

* (It's generally much easier when talking about food waste to use volume rather than weight measurements, as food waste densities vary so much – from 1 litre being equivalent to 1 kilo to a litre being less than half a kilo in weight. Wood chip also varies according to moisture content, the size of chip and the type of wood, but a litre could weigh around a quarter of a kilo.)

Ridan – a hand-powered in-vessel composter for food waste.

Pros of hand-powered turning mechanism models

- Much cheaper that the electrically driven machines.
- Can compost large amounts of food waste quickly without flies, smell or rodent problems.
- Continuous throughput.
- Does not require a building to house it.
- Does not need to be connected to a power supply.
- Great at mixing and getting compost through the thermophilic 'hot phase' of composting.

Cons of hand-powered turning mechanism models

- Price – although much cheaper to buy and run than the powered machines.
- Needs more attention than a powered machine.
- Needs a supply of dry woodchip.
- Can take quite a time for those using it to get it right.

Cost
£2,100.

Where to get one
Ridan Composting (www.ridan.co.uk).

Vertical composters

Vertical composting units (VCUs) are for much larger volumes of materials, collected on a municipal level.

How it works

Vertical composters use gravity to mix and aerate the contents. They use the heat generated to naturally pull air through the materials, and the compost can be continually harvested at the bottom. The vertical composting unit (VCU) has a mixing reception chamber on the ground, and the materials are taken up by elevator to start the composting process at the top of the unit. Fairfield Community Composting in Manchester uses this New-Zealand-designed machine; see www.fairfieldcompost.co.uk for more on this project.

Proper Job in Chagford, Devon, made its own versions of this idea first by adapting old chest freezers, then by using insulated panels on top of a series of paddles, which held the material back until they were rotated for harvesting.

Cost

The Proper Job large prototype costs around £2,000 to build.

The VCUs cost £100,000-200,000 with all the associated equipment, conveyors, macerators, etc.

Pros of vertical composters

- Gravity does the hard work.
- Continuous throughput.
- Smaller footprint, as it's vertical.

Cons of vertical composters

- You have to get the material up there – usually with conveyor belts.
- Accessibility.
- Cost.

Where to get one

VCU Europa (www.vcutechnology.com). If you are keen to build your own model, contact Proper Job (see Resources) for advice. The Association for Organics Recycling (www.organics-recycling.org.uk) can also give advice on larger-scale composting systems.

Static-pile systems

As with vertical composting units, static pile systems are for large volumes of materials, collected on a municipal level.

How it works

These large municipal systems blow or suck air through the materials. In one system the materials are heaped on to a perforated floor, then covered with a breathable membrane, such as Gortex, and then air is sucked through. Other systems have tunnels or large chambers and again the material is piled in and air is blown through perforated pipes.

Cost

Variable – these are usually bespoke systems for local authorities.

Pros of static-pile systems

- Designed specifically for the quantities of materials anticipated.

- Simpler technology than compost machines that tumble or turn the materials.

- Accessible at all times.

Cons of static-pile systems

- Large batch systems, so difficulty in maintaining consistency.

- Experience of building heaps needed.

- If a batch fails materials often need to be landfilled.

- Needs large concrete pads outside to build windrows to mature.

Where to get one

Anyone interested in finding out more about these larger-scale composting technologies should contact the Association for Organics Recycling (www.organics-recycling.org.uk), which publishes a producers' guidebook.

Maturation units (including 'worm pods')

By using secure (rat-proof) maturation containers you can dramatically increase the throughput of any in-vessel system, which means that your investment in any machine can be reduced, i.e. you can buy a smaller, less expensive model, because you can take out the composting materials that have been through the hottest phase of composting but are still only partially broken down and leave them to mature in simple, static maturation units.

Maturation units should become invaded by worms and can also be used as general-purpose composters. They are particularly useful for composting paper and card – for instance, paper towels. But because the paper and card is so absorbent you must be careful not to dry the compost out too much, so you will probably need to water the heaps. Worms are good at breaking down paper and card, given enough time. Leave materials to mature for six months to a year.

How it works

Since the material from an in-vessel system has been beautifully mixed up, all you have to do is put it in the maturation unit. If it is too dry then you can water it, or if too wet you can add some absorbent material; this is a good time to add paper and cardboard, as long as you make sure that the moisture levels are high enough.

In-vessel composters are capable of producing finished compost, but while they are great at accelerating the composting process through the warm and hot phases of composting, and you do get a stable product that could be used as a mulch, it is generally agreed that it is better to leave this material to mature, preferably to allow worms to work it through and fungi to break down the tougher, woody materials.

Scotty's Hot Box

The Scotty's Hot Box was designed as a maturation unit but can also be used as a 'one stop' composter for a variety of materials. I've used it for food waste, humanure and general garden clippings. It has a snugly fitting lid and a screwed-on base which is impenetrable by rodents if set up on a hard surface such as paving slabs, yet worms can squeeze their way in and thrive. Because of its generous capacity and double-skinned walls it maintains its self-generated warmth and can be both a hot compost bin and a wormery. The worms burrow down if it gets too hot for them and come back up when the heat abates.

Cost
£445.

Where to get one
Available from Proper Job Ltd (www.proper-job.org).

Scotty's Hot Box – a cubic-metre bin. The right-hand picture shows the front removed and the compost at the bottom ready to be harvested.

Pros of Scotty's Hot Box

- Large size coupled with hollow-board construction means it retains heat well.

- Worms love it – makes an excellent wormery and the worms cannot drown in it.

- Works well as a maturation box for many schools, businesses and institutions, and with any of the above in-vessel systems.

- Can be used as a general-purpose composter for any compost-able material.

- You can collect the leachate from it.

- If set up on a solid base then rats find it extremely hard to break in, although for food waste it is best used as a maturation bin than as a whole-composting system.

Cons of Scotty's Hot Box

- Price (bespoke handmade product).

- Size – much larger than a 'dalek'.

- Needs a fairly flat, level site.

Home-made maturation bays/bins/containers

If you make your own containers for the maturation phase it is advisable to be sure they are rat-proof – although there shouldn't be anything that rats will be interested in eating, they nevertheless love a warm place to burrow and nest, especially in the winter.

Maturation bays or containers can be made using brick or concrete blocks on a secure base of concrete or paving slabs, using the New-Zealand-box-type design (See Chapter 4, page 44). Use hefty boards such as scaffold boards for the front panels, and you will need to make snugly fitting lids as well. The advantage of making your own bays is that you can scale the size of the containers to the size of your operation and make as many as you need.

You could make the whole structure out of wood but would need to line it with weldmesh to stop rats gnawing their way in.

Cost

If using recycled materials, the bays could be free apart from the labour costs – otherwise cost obviously depends on the price of materials and the size of the bays.

Pros of home-made bays

- You can tailor the maturation bays to the size of your system.

- You can use recycled and/or reused materials and save on costs.

Cons of home-made bays

- Time, expertise and labour in construction.

- Cost of materials.

- You have to construct and leave in situ – not easily moveable.

Worm pods

Research carried out at the Worm Research Centre has led to the development of a fully integrated, purpose-designed worm bed.

How it works

Worm pods are capable of processing a wide range of materials from various waste streams, and are best used as a maturation unit for materials coming from an in-vessel composter. The pods are first loaded with a layer of bedding into which the worms are added, then thin layers of fresh food waste or thicker layers of pre-composted food waste can be added. The pods have a large surface area because worms will work just below the surface and so can spread themselves out further the larger the surface area. Given enough space, daily batches of waste can be placed in adjacent parts of the pods, giving worms time to work through one batch of material at a time. Because the pods are modular in design more pods can be added if needed to deal with increasing amounts of waste.

Cost
Small units for schools or demonstration
1.5 square metres: £300.
3kg worms: £60.
Drainage tank: £20.
Bedding: £20.

Large units
10 square metres: £1,500.
20kg worms: £400.
Drainage tank: £125.
Bedding: £75.

Pros of worm pods

- Modular in nature and can be used as a stand-alone operation or as a maturation stage for an in-vessel composting or anaerobic digestion.
- Purpose-designed system.
- Made of high-quality recycled plastic, coloured green to blend into the landscape better.
- Light, strong and durable.
- Integral drainage system – total leachate control.
- Easy to deliver and assemble.
- Well insulated.
- Height enables easy mechanical filling.

Cons of worm pods

- Large footprint – takes up more space than other composting systems.
- Security – more accessible than other composting systems to unwanted furry visitors.

Where to get one

Available from the Worm Research Centre (www.wormresearchcentre.co.uk).

CHAPTER 10

COMPOSTING IN SCHOOLS

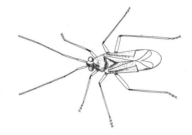

Schools are increasingly becoming involved in the environmental agenda, developing gardens, growing food, cooking healthy meals, procuring locally grown food and teaching children about how their food is produced and where it comes from. Schools are also investigating alternative energy and reducing their waste, and composting is a natural part of this commitment to both enhance garden areas and reduce waste.

Many organisations exist to help schools, e.g. Waste Watch, Global Action Plan, Eco-Schools, Resource Futures (see Resources section). In addition, community composting groups as well as Transition Towns and climate-change/low-carbon groups, in which there is a huge surge of interest, are often involved in helping their local schools to achieve their environmental aims.

The government's fruit scheme, which enables many primary school children to get some fresh fruit every day, has meant that the schools have had all the peels and cores to dispose of – or compost. Using the right systems this volume of 'putrescible' waste is easily converted into compost for the garden. However, what often happens is that schools struggle with inadequate composters and end up with plagues of fruit flies.

If you are a parent, governor or teacher, you might want to start a composting system or get a better system going at your school.

When my children were at primary school I persuaded the headmaster to let me set up a composting system for all the food waste. Rather reluctantly, he finally allowed me to do this. At the time I was involved with a project collecting food waste from about 50 households and had evolved a safe way of composting this material using old chest freezers and mixing the material with woodchip. So we set up two specially adapted chest freezers on blocks and the kitchen staff started putting their food waste into the freezers. The first freezer was designated as a 'first-stage hot composter' and the second one, which had worms in it, as a slower maturation composter. I had impressed upon the staff the need to contact me if they were not happy with any aspect of the set-up and I tried to monitor it myself as best as I could.

At first all went pretty much according to plan, but I was surprised to see that the material, instead of composting, just seemed to grow 'fur'. This puzzled me until I realised that the school did not do any fresh preparation on site – all the food was brought to the school ready-prepared as part of the 'chill chain' system. As a result there were very few bacteria in the freezers and so composting was not happening. A quick dollop of compost from my actively composting home system soon got the process moving.

Unfortunately, towards the end of the summer term, when I had stopped checking up on the process so often, materials started to be put directly into the second freezer – the wormery system – which wasn't designed as a 'hot composting' container and as a result odours started to be very noticeable and the kitchen staff became very upset. Instead of contacting me they just wanted to stop the whole thing and write it off as a failure.

This experience in the late 1990s certainly impressed on me how not to do things! And the world has changed since then; we are so much more aware of the urgent need to stop being so wasteful and to lessen our carbon footprint as much as possible. Also, there are compost containers now on the market that are capable of composting food waste without having to resort to the rather unsightly chest freezers in the school grounds that I was using back then.

Why compost at school?

Go into just about any school and, if you poke around, you will invariably see industrial-sized wheelie bins bulging with black sacks full of mixed rubbish. These are taken off, at a price, and generally buried in a landfill site or incinerated. Nearly all of this is material could be reused, recycled or composted to reduce the school's impact on the environment.

In schools the largest fraction of the waste stream consists of paper towels, paper, cardboard and compostable material. Reusing paper that still has one good clean side is an easy step, and much of the rest can be recycled. Some of the cardboard, soiled scrap paper and paper towels can be composted, although you have to be careful not to put paper and card – particularly large amounts – into tumbling systems, but they can go into maturation bays if these are well watered. The compostable material comprises leftover food, trimmings from food preparation, fruit cores and peelings, plant material from the grounds, grass cuttings, prunings, hedge clippings, etc. The problem is that the average 'dalek' composter is not up to the task of composting school waste efficiently. Experiences of schools trying to use these have shown that they quickly get filled up and overwhelmed with dense, oozy, sticky fruity waste, and attract fruit flies.

Schools that have tried to compost are often put off by these early experiences and certainly recoil in horror at the thought of dealing with food wastes such as mashed potato, gravy and custard. But with the right system and advice, schools can transform even these unlikely substances into lovely sweet-smelling compost and do their bit for the environment.

Tumbling compost bins are great fun to use as well as making fabulous compost.

Food-waste reduction ideas

Some schools are now trialling the Swedish system of letting primary school children help themselves to food. This way they take what they will actually eat rather than having that dictated to them by the dinner staff. This can result in less food being cooked in the first place and less to compost.

Some schools prepare the fruit break snacks too: cutting fruit up into bite-sized pieces makes it easier for the children to eat, gives them more choice and means there is less wastage.

One school I visited was making juice from fresh fruit at its sports day, and some of the children, who had never eaten fruit, loved the juice and were excitedly running to get their parents to try this wondrous nectar.

What to do with paper towels

Schools generate large amounts of used paper towels, which always present a challenge to compost, partly because of the sheer volume, and partly because they do not add structure to the composting mix (you need woodchip for that). The first step is always reduction – a new campaign to get children to shake water

Jora 270 bins at Ilfracombe School. These are set up on blocks so that a wheelbarrow can go underneath.

off their hands first is already reducing paper towel use.

Schools tell me that the coloured paper towels do not compost as well as the simple unbleached sort, so maybe just by procuring the right towels you can solve part of the problem.

A large volume of any one type of material, whether autumn leaves or paper towels, always needs careful consideration. Both paper towels and leaves are high in carbon and are dry and absorbent. So they need mixing with something green – high in nitrogen and wet. However, paper towels do not add structure to a bin and so quickly mat together. They don't work well in tumbling systems or continuous throughput systems, as they tend to ball up or clog the mechanism.

Paper towels do break down in a maturation system, albeit slowly. Worms like eating paper and card, but it has to be moist; so as long as it's well mixed with food waste or grass cuttings it will make good compost.

- If the school also has lots of grass cuttings to deal with, you could make simple containers or New-Zealand-type bins to layer grass with paper towels.

- Alternatively, you can layer them with the half-rotted food waste coming out of the tumbler or throughput system, e.g. the Ridan (see Chapter 9) and put in a maturation box.

- Make sure the mix is wet enough, as the paper towels will absorb a lot of moisture, so you will probably need to water it.

Research idea: growing fungi on paper towels

This is one approach to using up those paper towels. Fungi break down cellulose, which is in the paper. The towels should be wetted with rainwater and then seeded with commercially bought fungal spawn, such as oyster mushrooms. Fungi are amazing at cleaning up contaminated materials (see *Bioremediation* in the A–Z Guide), and so you can safely eat any of the fruiting mushrooms even if there have been pathogens on the paper towels. I don't know of anyone who has actually tried this yet but Paul Stamets (see Websites in Resources section) is a great enthusiast for using unusual materials to grow fungi and has a photo of one of his fungi books with fungi growing out of it!

Getting a school scheme started

First, it is important to do your homework.

1. Check out the organisations that can help (see Resources section).

2. The whole school community really needs to support the initiative. Get the headteacher, the caretaker and preferably all the staff (both teaching and ancillary), as well as the children, on board.

3. Check with the local authority to see whether it can offer any support, whether financial or practical.

4. Contact the relevant councillor. Councillors have money each year to spend on their wards and are often very keen to help the schools on their patch.

5. Undertake a waste audit – see below.

6. Make a plan and cost it out – see opposite.

7. Implement the plan – after raising the funds – see overleaf.

Conducting a waste audit

A waste audit of the whole school is the usual first step to get an idea of what is actually going into those wheelie bins.

1. Find out whether your council has a contract with any of the agencies listed in the Resources section, such as Waste Watch, Global Action Plan or Resource Futures.

2. Your local council may even offer to undertake the audit. If not, you will either have to undertake it yourselves or pay for it to be done.

3. The waste audit involves saving all the waste for a week and sorting it into all the different types, e.g:

   a) paper – this can be further sorted into white paper, coloured paper and paper towels

   b) card – cardboard packaging and thin card

   c) cans and bottles (there's usually very little, if any, glass at schools for recycling)

   d) plastic – bottles, containers and other plastic (cling film, etc.)

   e) food – packed-lunch waste, kitchen raw fruit and vegetable preparations, plate scrapings and leftover food

   f) other – this can be a large category in schools: anything from pencils and rulers to broken or redundant items of furniture or equipment

   g) residual, unsorted materials. These will generally end up in 'landfill'.

4. All the different types are then weighed, and it's noted what is already being recycled, how much more could be reused or recycled, and the amounts that could be composted.

Making a plan and costing it out

The most important first step is to simply reduce the amount of waste. With a little thought, instead of mixing up different materials they can be kept separate and thus easily recycled. This dramatically reduces the amount of waste going to landfill.

1. Set up containers/collection points for different materials; for instance, it's common for a lot of paper to be thrown away after only one side has been used, and boxes could be provided in every classroom for good clean paper that is used on only one side. Paper towels are often a significant part of a school's waste and, although they are compostable, they can quickly over-whelm a composting system – see 'What to do with paper towels', page 170.

Work out how many collection points and containers you need and how much they will cost.

2. Just by doing the waste audit you will find out just how much food, and what sort, is being wasted, and that in itself can inform the catering staff how to prevent some wastage.

3. The remaining food waste can be composted using an appropriate system as long as the school has enough space to use the resulting compost. This of course will have significant cost implications. A very small primary school may need to use only the domestic-type food-waste composting systems (depending of course on the amounts of food waste detailed in the waste audit), as described in Chapter 4. Medium-sized primary schools will need a tumbling composter and a good secure maturation unit. Larger primary schools will need more than one tumbler, or a larger composter such as the Ridan, and more space for maturation units. Secondary schools and community colleges will need to consider getting one of the larger in-vessel systems. (See Chapter 9 for all these larger systems.)

4. Decide where to locate the composting system, and remember that you will need a supply of dry wood chippings, so a container for those will need to be factored into any scheme. The local authority may be able to supply wood chippings, or ask the parents, staff and PTA if they know any tree surgeons, etc. who may be able to supply woodchip. Alternatively, ask any local tree/garden/landscaping businesses that might be happy to supply the odd load. You can also use sawdust, but use only sawdust from sources using 100-per-cent untreated wood – preferably softwood – and avoid sawdust made from materials such as MDF, as it will contain some pretty nasty noxious substances.

5. Find out how much the school is paying for its waste collection and how much could be saved by composting. This saving can help fund the scheme over time.

6. Write a budget to cover all the changes you would like to implement

Implementing the plan

1. The system has to be taken on by the whole school and so it is important that, right from the start, it is not going to be reliant on one member of staff having to manage the scheme as an extracurricular activity.

2. Headteachers can rewrite staff contracts to enable key members of staff to be 'compost champions' – to spend time fundraising, overseeing and running

the day-to-day process – or just change the caretaker's contract to include recycling and composting in the duties.

3. The system can be incorporated into the curriculum in many ways, and many of the external agencies listed in the Resources section can offer suggestions and examples of how to do this.

4. Children need to understand why composting (and recycling) are being introduced, or further enhanced, in their school; how composting works; and how they are going to be involved practically in the scheme. This is where the external agencies can be very useful.

5. Children should be involved in the day-to-day running of the system. Forming a 'Little Rotters' club is one way to do it – see www.littlerotters.org.uk. This website also lists many other organisations that can be useful.

6. Whole learning communities can be involved in larger joined-up schemes, as has happened with the 'Growing our Future' project in West Devon, where eleven primary schools and the community college are all involved in a very exciting project. A more joined-up project like this, which involves food procurement, renewable energy, artwork, events involving the parents and local residents, visiting speakers, performers and workshop days in schools, takes a lot more funding and organising on the one hand, but it also ticks so many funding 'boxes' that it is likely to be of great interest to potential funders.

7. Make a funding strategy plan – start with 'blue sky' thinking where anything goes – let your imagination soar! Then break your ideas down into bite-sized fundable chunks.

8. Make a list of potential funders. Include the school itself as number one on the list – funders are going to be impressed by the school's commitment if it has already raised or committed money towards the project. Put down any ideas for 'in kind' commitment that could be provided by the school, PTA or local volunteers.

9. When looking for funders, start locally:

   a) your councils, e.g. parish, district, county (at the very least they should be able to signpost you towards some relevant funders)

   b) your local councillors – they have money to spend on their patch

   c) local businesses.

10. Then look at other funders – but always check the criteria that the funders specify and don't bother trying to get a project funded that doesn't meet their criteria.

Summary

Getting things really happening at the school depends on some key factors being in place.

*   The whole school community really needs to support the initiative.

*   Children and staff in the school need to have some compost training so that everyone understands the key concepts of composting.

*   The kitchen staff have to be willing to separate out the compostable materials and not put plastics and other rubbish in the compost caddy bins.

*   Each classroom needs caddies for fruit-break waste and tuck-shop waste, and the children have to understand exactly what they can put in the caddies to go to the compost bins.

*   A 'eco' or 'Little Rotters' team needs to be set up to do the day-to-day work of emptying these caddies – see www.littlerotters.org.uk for a free useful pack.

*   Key staff members must to be able to champion the scheme and do quite a bit of work. Ideally their contracts will be altered so they are given paid time to look after the compost system.

*   Schools will probably need funding for the composting equipment and its set-up. Composting equipment suitable for food waste composting is expensive, e.g. the set-up cost for a Jora 270 and Scotty's Hot Box is over £800. Ideally the local authority will also support the scheme financially.

*   There must be suitable areas for both the composting and the subsequent use of the finished compost.

*   There must be a good supply of sawdust, woodchip or shredded hedge prunings, etc. so that food waste can be blended with carbon in the best form to make the compost properly – it may be necessary to buy in the woodchip, but often the local council can oblige, or a parent/governor may have a supply of shredded green waste or chippings.

Composting in schools is an idea whose time has come. Jeanette Orrey and Jamie Oliver have started the food culture revolution in schools, and more and more schools are starting to create gardens. If we continually remove crops from the soil without putting anything back, the humus in the soil gradually becomes exhausted. By composting, a whole cycle of fertility is maintained, with the compost being returned to the soil to feed the plants and to build humus – which is why it is so important to compost everything we can.

Weighing the canteen waste at Ilfracombe School.

RESOURCES

Books

Composting

Gershuny, Grace and Martin, Deborah L. (eds) (1992) *The Rodale Book of Composting*. Rodale Press, distributed by Eco-logic Books. Originally published in 1979 by Jerry Minnich, Marjorie Hunt and the editors of *Organic Gardening* magazine, this is probably one of the best books about composting.

Pears, Pauline (1999) *All About Compost: Recycling household and garden waste*. Search Press. Also available from the Organic Gardening catalogue (see Garden Organic, page 185).

Pears, Pauline (2009) *The Garden Organic guide to Making Compost*. Search Press.

The Community Composting Network (2006) *The Community Composting Guide*.

Human waste composting

Harper, Peter and Halestrap, Louise (2001) *Lifting the Lid: An ecological approach to toilet systems*. Centre for Alternative Technology.

Jenkins, Joe (2005, 3rd edn) *The Humanure Handbook*. Jenkins Publishing, distributed by Green Books.

King, Franklin H. (1911) *Farmers of Forty Centuries*. Dover Publications. A classic.

Moodie, Mark (1996) *Flowforms (Human Waste, the Universe and Everything)*. Eco-logic books.

Steinfeld, Carol (2004) *Liquid Gold: The lore and logic of using urine to grow plants*. Green Books.

Soil and humus

Faber and Faber has a huge back catalogue of books often found in second-hand bookshops; keep an eye out too for the Lanthorn Press. Some are classics, which have been kept in print. Look out particularly for anything by:

Balfour, Lady Eve, e.g. *The Living Soil*, first published 1943, Faber and Faber; reprinted by Soil Association Classics, 2006. Distributed by Green Books.

Bruce, Maye E., e.g. *Common-Sense Compost Making*, published 1950. Faber and Faber.

Pfeiffer, Ehrenfried, e.g. *Soil Fertility*, first published 1947, revised 2008. Lanthorn Press.

Howard, Sir Albert, e.g. *An Agricultural Testament* (OUP 1945), *Farming and Gardening for Health or Disease* (Faber and Faber, 1945; also reprinted by Soil Association Classics, 2006, distributed by Green Books) and *Soil and Health* (Faber and Faber, 1945). These are all classics and well worth reading.

Sykes, Friend, e.g. *Humus and the Farmer*, published 1946. Faber and Faber.

Other soil and humus books

Bruges, James (2009) *Biochar*. Green Books.

Gershuny, Grace and Smillie, Joe (2008, fourth edn) *The Soul of Soil*. Chelsea Green.

Nardi, James B. *Life in the Soil: A guide for naturalists and gardeners* (2007) University of Chicago Press.

Tompkins, Peter and Bird, Christopher (1998) *The Secrets of the Soil*. Arkana.

Worms

Appelhof, Mary (1997, second edn) *Worms eat my Garbage*. Eco-logic Books.

Darwin, Charles (1883) *Vegetable Mould and Earthworms*. John Murray.

Pilkington, G. (2005) *Composting with Worms*. Eco-logic Books.

Other recommended reads

Dowding, Charles (2007) *Organic Gardening: The natural no-dig way*. Green Books.

Stamets, Paul (2004) *Mycelium Running: How mushrooms can help save the world*. Ten Speed Press. (Look out also for other books by Paul Stamets.)

Fukuoka, Masanobu (1978, Rodale Press) *The One Straw Revolution*. Now published by New York Review of Books Classics.

Hopkins, Rob (2008) *The Transition Handbook: From oil dependency to local resilience.* Green Books.

Pinkerton, Tamzin and Hopkins, Rob (2009) *Local Food: How to make it happen in your community.* Green Books.

Websites

Biochar

http://terrapreta.bioenergylists.org
The rediscovery of using charcoal as a soil improvement has resulted in enormous interest in carrying out research projects of all kinds. For a wealth of information have a look at this site.

Compost

See also under 'Organisations', page 182, for many more suggestions.

http://compost.css.cornell.edu/Composting_homepage.html
The Cornell University compost website. I have visited it regularly and it's a great source of information.

www.gardenorganic.org.uk
As an ex-Henry-Doubleday student and member I regularly visit the Garden Organic website. If you are not a member of Garden Organic have a look and browse the excellent catalogue.

http://journeytoforever.org
This very comprehensive site has lots of links to interesting projects and information on organic growing and composting, and includes some excellent information on composting and compost reads. See reviews and précis accounts of books, and information on composting, in the 'small farms library' section.

http://whatcom.wsu.edu/ag/compost/
The Washington State University website, which I have found to be very useful.

www.biocycle.net/
If you want to find out about large-scale composting in the States then BioCycle is

for you. I used to subscribe to *BioCycle* magazine and it does include some interesting material, although it's mostly geared to the really big compost makers.

Community composting

See under Community Composting Network in 'Organisations'.

Compost teas

www.attra.org/attra-pub/compost-tea-notes.html#compostteas
This is a great place to start, with masses of information about compost tea and compost extracts, including slide shows and articles.

Composting in schools

www.littlerotters.org.uk
The Little Rotters site provides information about composting in schools with masses of classroom activities, and includes a free downloadable pack.

Fungi

www.fungi.com
Paul Stamets' website. If you want to find out all about fungi – how to grow edible and medicinal fungi and how they are used in 'mycoremediation', i.e. cleaning up polluted soils, then look at this website and get hold of Paul Stamets' books. Very inspirational.

No-dig

www.charlesdowding.co.uk
Charles Dowding is a very experienced organic grower who doesn't dig! His website is very well laid out and a mine of information, just like his excellent books, and includes details of the courses he regularly runs.

Rock dust

www.seercentre.org.uk
The Seer centre in Scotland has great claims about using rock dust, both to improve soils and crops and also to help combat climate change. It has been

strongly endorsed by Graham Harvey in his excellent book *We Want Real Food*.

Soil food web – Elaine Ingham

www.soilfoodweb.com
Elaine Ingham has produced many lectures on soil, compost tea and compost, which you can buy from this site. (She has written the definitive guide on compost tea brewing – but you can also find out about brewing compost tea on YouTube.)

Transition Network

www.transitiontowns.org
www.transitionculture.org
www.transitionbooks.net
The Transition movement is a global network of initiatives to raise awareness of and respond to the challenges of peak oil and climate change. The movement is growing really fast and much of its work is focused on growing food locally – and that, of course, involves making compost.

Zoo poo

www.ecosci.co.uk/zoopoo.php
Zoo animals produce a lot of poo. At Paignton Zoo they compost the large herbivore poo and make great compost! Paignton Zoo was a Devon Environmental Business Initiative (DEBI) award winner in 2008.

Organisations

Association for Organics Recycling
3 Burystead Place
Wellingborough
Northamptonshire NN8 1AH
0870 160 3270
www.organics-recycling.org.uk
Formerly The Composting Association, this is the UK's not-for-profit membership organisation promoting the sustainable management of biodegradable resources. It actively promotes the use of biological treatment techniques, and encourages good management practices throughout the industry.

Biodynamic Agricultural Association (BDAA)
Painswick Inn
Stroud
Gloucestershire GL5 1QG
01453 759501
www.biodynamic.org.uk
The BDAA is founded on a holistic and spiritual understanding of nature and the human being's role within it. At its heart is the idea of the farm as a self-contained evolving organism, whose life relies on home-produced compost manures and animal feeds, with minimum external inputs.

Centre for Alternative Technology
Machynlleth
Powys SY20 9AZ
01654 705950
www.cat.org.uk
The Centre for Alternative Technology has been going since 1973 – you can find out how it has grown since then and browse through its excellent shop at this website. CAT's biology department has done much pioneering research in composting and food growing and has produced excellent publications on composting, compost toilets, grey water systems and much more.

Community Composting Network (CCN)
67 Alexandra Road
Sheffield S2 3EE
0114 258 0483
www.communitycompost.org
The Community Composting Network supports and promotes the community management and use of waste biodegradable resources. Projects range in scale, from individuals or small groups working on allotment sites or promoting home composting to social enterprises with local authority contracts providing kerbside collection services.

Also see **www.growingwithcompost.org**. This website show what is happening across Europe and has some useful downloadable documents.

The Community Composting Network has been working with the New Economics Foundation and The Open University. **www.valuingcommunitycomposting.org.uk/page.cfm** provides a 'Toolkit for unlocking the potential of community composting', which shows just how important community composting projects can be to their communities and how they can develop into so many other areas.

Compost Doctors
c/o CRN UK
57 Prince Street
Bristol BS1 4QH
01872 560443
www.compostdoctors.org.uk

Compost Doctors is a consortium of experienced, professional composters specialising in small-scale, on-site composting of food waste. Sharing case studies and experiences of on-site composting, the group has built up a unique body of expertise, ranging from equipment to legislation. It provides consultancy to all kinds of catering establishments, from pubs, hotels and visitor attractions to prisons and hospitals.

Defra (the Department for Environment, Food and Rural Affairs)
Nobel House
17 Smith Square
London SW1P 3JR
0845 933 5577
www.defra.gov.uk
Government department that deals with food, air, land, water, people, animals and plants. Contact it or see its website for advice, including advice on the safe disposal of pernicious weeds.

Devon Community Composting Network
c/o Proper Job, Crannafords Business Park
Market field, Chagford
Devon TQ13 8DJ
01647 432923
www.dccn.org.uk
This network actually predates the national Community Composting Network and is funded by Devon local authorities who all work together on waste, recycling and composting issues. It works to support community groups and to help schools compost food waste.

Eco-Schools

England:
Keep Britain Tidy
Elizabeth House
The Pier, Wigan WN3 4EX
01942 612621
www.eco-schools.org.uk

Wales:
c/o Keep Wales Tidy
33-35 Cathedral Road
Cardiff CF11 9HB
See website for the appropriate telephone number for your area
www.eco-schoolswales.org

Scotland:
c/o Keep Scotland Beautiful
Wallace House, 17-21 Maxwell Place
Stirling FK8 1JU
01786 468234
www.ecoschoolsscotland.org

Northern Ireland:
TIDY Northern Ireland
Bridge House, Paulett Avenue
Belfast BT5 4HD
028 9073 6920
www.eco-schools.org.uk

Environment Agency
Phone 08708 506506 to find the address of your regional centre.
www.environment-agency.gov.uk
The Environment Agency is responsible for protecting and improving the environment in England and Wales. Contact it or see its excellent website for advice on the safe disposal of non-compostable materials, including pernicious weeds. You need to contact the Environment Agency if you want to start a community composting scheme – but talk to the Community Composting Network first.

Garden Organic
Ryton-on-Dunsmore
Coventry CV8 3LG
02476 303517
www.homecomposting.org.uk
www.gardenorganic.org.uk
www.organiccatalogue.com (for its catalogue)
This used to be called the HDRA (Henry Doubleday Research Association). Garden Organic is dedicated to researching and promoting organic gardening, farming and food. It also runs the master composter programme.

Global Action Plan
8 Fulwood Place
London WC1V 6HG
020 7405 5633
www.globalactionplan.org.uk
Delivers 'waste'-related work in schools, including composting and teacher training.

Resource Futures
CREATE Centre   and: 3rd Floor, Munro House
Smeaton Road   Duke Street
Bristol BS1 6XN   Leeds, LS9 8AG
0117 930 4355   0113 243 8777
www.resourcefutures.co.uk
Also delivers 'waste'-related work in schools, including composting and teacher training.

Soil Association
South Plaza
Marlborough Street
Bristol BS1 3NX
0117 314 5000
www.soilassociation.org
The Soil Association was founded in 1946 by a group of far-sighted individuals who were concerned about the health implications of increasingly intensive agri-

cultural systems following the Second World War. Now, through its 'Food for life' partnerships, it is committed to transforming food culture by, for example, revolutionising school meals to be fresh, local and organic, and inspiring families and communities to grow and cook food.

Waste and Resources Action Programme (WRAP)

The Old Academy
21 Horse Fair, Banbury
Oxon OX16 0AH
Home composting helpline: 0845 600 0323
www.wrap.org.uk
The WRAP Home Composting Scheme works with local authorities and other selected organisations to promote home composting. It encourages people to purchase compost bins at a subsidised price. Advice and support is also provided for all households engaging in home composting, via support materials, a dedicated helpline and advisors in the field.

Waste Watch

56-64 Leonard Street
London EC2A 4LT
020 7549 0300
www.wastewatch.org.uk
A UK environmental charity working to change the way people use the world's natural resources. It delivers 'waste'-related lessons, including composting work, in schools, and is also involved in training teachers. A wealth of information is available for subscriber schools.

The Worm Research Centre

Phoenix Farm
Asselby, Howden
East Yorkshire
DN14 7HF
01757 630456
www.wormresearchcentre.co.uk
The Worm Research Centre (WRC) is also the home of 'Green Machine Solutions'. Steve Ross-Smith and Nicky Scott collaborated on the design of the 'Scotty's Hot Box' and the 'Scotspin', and Green Machine manufactures these products as well as Worm Pods, Worm Bags and compost screening equipment. Nicky, Steve and Carly Ross-Smith of WRC are 'Compost Doctors', and Steve and Carly also work with the Open University on worm research.

Equipment

General

A wide range of composters is available from many online retailers, and you can usually order either online or by phone. The following is just a selection.

Green Gardener
01603 715096, www.greengardener.co.uk

Green and Easy
0845 257 0550, www.greenandeasy.co.uk

Green Fingers
0845 345 0728, www.greenfingers.com

Original Organics
0808 120 9676, www.originalorganics.co.uk

Recycle Works
0800 032 0377, www.recycleworks.co.uk

Wiggly Wigglers
01981 500391, www.wigglywigglers.co.uk

You can also look at this section of the Waste and Resources Action Programme (WRAP) website: **www.recyclenow.com/home_composting/buy_a_bin**. WRAP was set up by the government to promote and encourage reuse, recycling and composting. It helps local authorities to promote home composting, and many councils work in partnership with WRAP and offer compost bins. See the website for a range of low-cost bins available in your area through this partnership and to see if your council is working with WRAP.

Garden-waste and raw-food-waste composters

Dalek bins
A lot of companies sell 'dalek'-type bins, they are available from garden centres and online. Also see the WRAP website (above) to find out what discounted dalek bins are available in your area.
Daleks come in different forms and vary in:

- size – round/conical bins from around 200 litres to 350 litres

- shape – some are taller (e.g. Garden King) and do not flare out at the base; some are conical in shape (e.g. Rotol); others are square in section, e.g. Thermo King (NB larger square bins fall into a separate category – see below)

- whether or not they have a hatch

- whether or not they have a (sometimes optional) base plate, e.g. Blackwall's 'compost converter' and 'compost machine', and the Thermo King

- colour: usually black or green but can have camouflage pattern too.

Square and other shaped plastic bins
These designs tend to be bigger than the dalek bins and have removable panels to access the compost. Some are made of thicker insulating plastic, e.g. Eco King and Thermo King made by Garantia, who also do a range of larger sizes with optional base plates. These bins can be obtained from online suppliers, e.g. Green Fingers or Gardeners' World (0845 224 1484, www.gardenersworld.net).

New Zealand boxes
Again, these are available from many sources, but two online suppliers that sell new Zealand boxes and much more are Wiggly Wigglers and Recycle Works.

Wooden slatted composters
Available from various online suppliers, including Recycle Works and Green Fingers.

Beehive composters
These are available from many online suppliers, including Wiggly Wigglers.

Small-scale vertical composting units
The Earthmaker unit is available from various online retailers, or direct from the manufacturer.
Earthmaker: 0870 728 0604, www.earthmaker.co.uk

Small-scale non-raw food-waste solutions

Green Johanna and Green Cone
Both available from Green Cone, as well as other online retailers.
Green Cone: 0800 731 2572, www.greencone.com

Tumblers
The smaller 'end over end' tumblers are often found in garden centres. Larger models are available online and through gardening catalogues. See also Scotspin and Jora models, page 155. The CompoSphere is available from online retailers including Original Organics.

Bokashi and Effective Microorganisms

Also available from Original Organics, Recycle Works, Living Soil (www.livingsoil.co.uk, orders online or by post) and West Country Worms (see 'Wormeries', below).

Wormeries

Lots of suppliers do wormeries – see 'General', page 187. The following are some specific ones.

Worms Direct: 01245 381933, www.wormsdirectuk.co.uk

West Country Worms: 01803 712738, www.westcountryworms.co.uk

Worm Hotel: 01263 587722, www.thewormhotel.com

Worm City: 08000 141598, www.wormcity.co.uk

You can also buy wooden wormeries, e.g. from Recycle Works.

For ideas on making your own wormery see www.wikihow.com/Make-Your-Own-Worm-Compost-System.

Rolypig and Rolymole

Both these systems are fun for kids in schools. The Rolypig is 'fed' with compost by lifting the snout. You roll the pig around a lawn and the material goes through an Archimedes screw, taking the material through several internal chambers before exiting into a drawer at the end, so it is a continuous throughput design. Because it is a completely contained system it is suitable for food waste. The Rolymole wormery is a continuous-throughput wormery – just wiggle the tail to harvest the finished compost.

Rolypig: 01398 361656, www.rolypig.com

Larger-scale food-waste composters

Scotty's Hot Box and the Scotspin

The **Worm Research Centre** and **Green Machine Solutions** (see 'Organisations', page 186)

Proper Job Ltd

Chagford, Devon

01647 432985

www.proper-job.org

Jora 125, 270, 400 and 5100

Smartsoil (UK agents for Joraform Sweden)

Neath, West Glamorgan

01639 701888

www.smartsoil.co.uk

Big Hanna
Big Hanna UK
Woodbridge, Suffolk
01728 685899
www.bighanna.co.uk

Rocket
Accelerated Compost
Macclesfield, Cheshire
01625 666790
www.quickcompost.co.uk

Ridan
Ridan Composting Ltd
Exmoor, Devon
01598 740075
www.ridan.co.uk

VCU
VCU Europa Ltd
Theale, Berkshire
0118 929 8266
www.vcutechnology.com

Static pile
Association for Organics Recycling
Wellingborough, Northamptonshire
08701 603270
www.organics-recycling.org.uk

Worm pods
The Worm Research Centre (see 'Organisations', page 186)

Other systems

Nature Mill composter

This composter from the USA is now being sold in Europe too. It's a miniature 'in-vessel' composting unit that is electrically powered and operates in your kitchen, producing finished compost in situ. See www.naturemill.com.

Other equipment

Wool insulation
100-per-cent natural biodegradable wool insulation, which you could use to wrap your compost bin up with, is available from Bellacouche (01647 432155, www. bellacouche.com).

Raised beds
Modular raised-bed sides are available from suppliers such as Garden Organic, Recycle Works, Green and Easy (see 'General', page 187) or Harrod Horticultural (0845 402 5300, www.harrodhorticultural.com).

INDEX

SALAD LEAVES FOR ALL SEASONS

Organic growing from pot to plot

Charles Dowding

How to grow healthy, tasty salad leaves, whatever the size of your growing space

"This is the number one book for anyone who loves salads." **Anna Pavord**

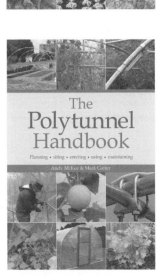

ORGANIC GARDENING

The Natural No-Dig Way

Charles Dowding

"One of our most respected vegetable growers . . . Now ordinary gardeners can benefit from his years of practical experience, growing great vegetables in harmony with Mother Earth." **Joy Larkcom**

THE POLYTUNNEL HANDBOOK

Andy McKee and Mark Gatter

The 'fifth season' in your garden – how to use a polytunnel to grow food all year round

"Polytunnels have a key role to play in the grow-your-own revolution, and a comprehensive guide such as this is long overdue." **Simon McEwan, Editor, *Country Smallholding***